C000131321

Beagles

The Owner's Guide from Puppy to Old Age

Choosing, Caring for, Grooming, Health, Training
and Understanding Your Beagle Dog or Puppy

By Alex Seymour

Copyright and Trademarks

All rights reserved. No part of this book may be reproduced or transferred in any form or by any means, graphic, electronic, or mechanical, including photocopying, recording, taping, or by any information storage retrieval system, without the written permission of the author. All products, publications, software and services mentioned and recommended in this publication are protected by trademarks. In such instance, all trademarks & copyright belong to the respective owners. A catalogue record for this book is available from the British Library.

This publication is Copyright © 2017 by CWP Publishing.

ISBN: 978-1-910677-11-7

Disclaimer and Legal Notice

This book has been written to provide useful information on the Beagle. It should not be used to diagnose or treat any medical condition. For diagnosis or treatment of any animal medical condition, consult a qualified veterinarian. The author and publishers are not responsible or liable for any specific health or allergy conditions that may require medical supervision and are not liable for any damages or negative consequences from any treatment, action, application, or preparation, to any person reading or following the information in this book. References are provided for informational purposes only and do not constitute endorsement of any websites or other sources mentioned. We have no control over the nature, content, and availability of the websites listed.

While every attempt has been made to verify the information shared in this book, neither the author nor the affiliates assume any responsibility for errors, omissions, or contrary interpretation of the subject matter herein. Any perceived slights to any specific person(s) or organization(s) are purely unintentional. The information in this book is not intended to serve as legal advice.

Foreword

Congratulations on purchasing this book. You've made a wise choice, as many of the world's top Beagle breeders have been involved in contributing to this book.

Once you've reached the end, you will have all the information you need to make a well-informed decision whether or not the Beagle is the breed for you. **Also, at the end, you will find a very special surprise in store as a thank you for buying this book!!!**

As an expert trainer and professional dog whisperer, I will teach you the human side of the equation, so you can learn how to think more like your Beagle and eliminate behavioral problems.

Beagles are proper little hounds in a compact, elegant package. Muscular, and handsome, especially in the classic tricolor coat with the black saddle and white-tipped tail, the Beagle is a dog bred to work. As you learn more about his breed history, you'll see that the Beagle's superior tracking abilities and energetic stamina were actively cultivated to match his prey of choice, hares and rabbits.

A less aristocratically inclined dog than the Foxhound and certainly more lively and energetic than the Basset Hound, the Beagle straddles the world of working and companion dog with lively aplomb. Although stubborn by nature, a Beagle can be an excellent family pet. This is only true, however, if you have the time and energy to meet his physical needs for exercise and his intellectual need for something interesting to do.

Although this is a book about keeping Beagles as pets, they are very much still working dogs, and they are still kept in packs for competition in field trials. You cannot "domesticate" the hunter and tracker from a Beagle.

If, however, you want an active, engaged, loyal, intelligent dog that is almost impossible to wear down, the Beagle could be exactly the pet for you and your family. Hard core devotees say there is no better dog, but this is not necessarily the breed for every household.

Acknowledgments

In writing this book, I also sought tips, advice, photos, and opinions from many experts on the Beagle breed. In particular, I wish to thank the following wonderful breeders, organizations, owners, and vets for their outstanding help and contribution:

United States and Canada Contributors

Ruth Darlene Stewart of Aladar Beagles
http://www.aladarbeagles.com/

Carol and Lori Norman of Lokavi Beagles
http://www.lokavi.com/

Bev Davies-Fraser of Waskasoo Kennel
http://waskasoo.weebly.com/

Joan Wurst of Everwind Beagles
http://www.everwindsaintsandbeagles.com/

Claudia Anderson of TwainHeart Beagles
http://www.twainheartbeagles.com/

Edy Ballard of Ironwood Beagles
https://www.ironwoodbeagles.com/

Sandra Groeschel of The Whim
Email: whim.beagles@gmail.com

Carol Herr of Roirdan Beagles
http://www.roirdanbeagles.com/

Alayne Mullen of Lane Rae Beagles
http://www.laneraebeagles.com/

Cindy Williams of Honey Pot Hounds
https://www.honeypothounds.com/

Mary Cummings and Sue Nichols of Stone Meadow & The Hounds of Lightfall - Email: stonemeadowkennel@yahoo.com

Patricia Eschbach of Spring Creek Beagles
http://www.springcreekbeagles.com/

Rachel Southammavong of South Beagles
https://www.facebook.com/southbeagles

Teresa (Teri) NeSmith of Encore Beagles
http://www.encorebeagles.com

Teresa Gaier of Copper Rose Beagles
http://www.copperrosebeagles.com/

Heather and Robert Lindberg of Windstar Beagles
Email: hlindberg928@gmail.com

Ann Roth of Hounds of Harnett (since 1979)
Email: harnetthounds@juno.com

Phyllis Wright of MPW
Email: pwright6131@earthlink.net

Lindsay Bryson of Allegro Beagles
http://www.allegrobeagles.webs.com

United Kingdom Contributors

Samantha Goldberg BVSc MRCVS
UK Beagle Clubs KC Health Co-ordinator
http://www.beaglehealth.info/
http://www.molesend.co.uk

Veronica and Rosie Longman of Chatoyant Beagles
Email: chatoyantbeagles@hotmail.co.uk

Peter and Val Davies of Barrvale Beagles
Email: barrvale@btinternet.com

Gary Clacher of Misken Beagles
Email: gary@misken.co.uk

Susie Arden of Madika Beagles
Email: susiearden@hotmail.co.uk

Hazel Deans of Gempeni Beagles
Email: hazel_deans@btinternet.com

Stacey Burrows of Summerlily Beagles
Email: summerlilybeagle@aol.co.uk

Natasha Bell of Alfadais Beagles
http://www.alfadaisbeagles.co.uk/

Andrew and Tanya Gittins of Boomerloo Beagles
Email: gittins158@btinternet.com

Sharon Hardisty of Blunderhall Beagles
http://www.blunderhallbeagles.co.uk/

Diana Brown of Raimex Beagles
Email: raimexbeagles@aol.com

FANCY SOME FUN? WE ALSO RECOMMEND BEAGLES GO AROUND THE WORLD COLOURING BOOK BY FEEL HAPPY COLOURING...

The top-selling coloring book for adult Beagle owners is available on Amazon and other good online bookstores.

This is a memorable gift idea even if you are not personally into coloring for relaxation, fun, and enjoyment.

Table of Contents

Table of Contents

Chapter 1 – Meet the Beagle

Beagles are hounds that were originally bred to be members of hunting packs. They are physically smaller than Foxhounds, and brighter and more energetic than Bassets, but once you hear a Beagle howl for the first time, you'll never doubt his hound lineage.

The name "Beagle" derives from the French "begueule" meaning "open throat" and the Gaelic "beag" for small. This breed can bay with the big dogs, however, this trait that can make them a challenge in an apartment setting if they haven't received proper training early in life.

Photo Credit: Mary Cummings and Sue Nichols of Stone Meadow & The Hounds of Lightfall.

The purpose of this book is to consider Beagles as family pets. In the United States, they are currently the fifth favorite companion breed.

Social, sweet, and gentle, they are enthusiastic and intelligent pets, with minimal grooming needs and an average life expectancy of 12–15 years.

Experienced Beagle breeders from all over the world have kindly given their time to answer questions and give their expert advice. You are about to benefit from literally hundreds of years' experience of breeding and living with Beagles.

We asked **Carol Herr of Roirdan Beagles** what, in her opinion, are the best things about the Beagle breed: "Besides being the cutest puppies, they are sweet, loveable, great lap dogs, and some even hug. They are naturally a pack dog, so they get along with others dogs. They have lots of energy, so get along great with children. They love toys, and will play catch and retrieve all by themselves. They are very smart and are very food motivated, making them easy to train. They will do most anything for food. Beagles are very expressive and can give you evil looks if not happy with the situation. They are little clowns, and you should have a sense of humor to own one."

Teresa (Teri) NeSmith of Encore Beagles adds: "As a Beagle breeder with over 40 years' experience in the breed, the most essential tip would be to expect the unexpected! Beagles are merry little hounds! They are nosey, love to play, and most of all they love attention and will do most anything to get it! Beagles make wonderful pets for the family!"

Sam Goldberg of Molesend Beagles: "My husband wanted a dog which had an interesting personality; we both spent time with Foxhounds as teenagers and wanted a smaller version of the hound without the ability to escape and climb fences!"

Beagle Breed History

Like many breeds, the exact origins of the Beagle are uncertain. As early as the 5th century BCE, however, hunting dogs of a similar description were being used in Greece. In the 8th century, the St. Hubert Hound, a scent dog, was used to create the Talbot Hound, a breed brought to England by William the Conqueror in the 11th century. To improve the dog's running abilities, they were crossed with Greyhounds.

Beagles are scent hounds ultimately refined for the specific purpose of hunting hares in England and Continental Europe. The dogs are the product of selective breeding programs covering centuries of development. Beagles are literally designed to hunt 8–10 pound / 3.6–4.5 kg hares and rabbits with the ability to reach speeds up to 40 mph / 64.37 kph over short distances.

Much of the Beagle's development occurred in England where hunting was rigidly controlled by class structure. Only the king could hunt deer. Nobles with the resources to keep horses and dogs had the option to go after fox. Lesser nobles, however, could only target quarry like hare.

The name Beagle was first used to describe a very small dog that stood just 8–9 inches / 20.32–22.86 cm tall. This miniature breed, sometimes called the Pocket Beagle, became extinct in 1901.

In the 18th century, two breeds, the Southern Hound and the North Country Beagle, were crossed with larger breeds to create the Foxhound, and in the 1840s, the standard Beagle.

Almost all Beagles today can trace their line back to the work of one enthusiast in England, Parson Honeywood, who formed a pack of North Country dogs in the mid-1800s. He is credited with combining and refining the best qualities of the Southern and North Country dogs.

The Foxhound and the Beagle developed contemporaneously to meet the requirements of different levels of the landed gentry. Additionally, the qualities desired in a Beagle depended on the prevailing quality of the hare population.

In times when hares were scarce, a keen nose that allowed the dog to follow one animal for an extended period to prolong the pleasure of the hunt for the hunters was valued. When hares were so plentiful as to be causing crop damage, dogs that were fast enough to catch as many of the vermin in one day as possible were more valuable.

By 1887, there were 18 packs of Beagles in England. The breed was imported to the United States in the early 1870s. One of the first dedicated enthusiasts was General Richard Rowett of Illinois. Rowett and others interested in the beauty and functionality of the dogs founded the National Beagle Club of America in 1884. The next year, the American Kennel Club recognized the breed.

The first Beagle field trial was held in Hyannis, Massachusetts in 1888, with the first specialty breed shows organized in 1891. The breed rapidly came to be prized both for its hunting abilities and its quality as a family dog.

The Beagle's heyday in the U.S. occurred in the 1940s and 1950s when there was still enough open country for sportsmen to use the dogs to hunt cottontail rabbits. Packs of Beagles competed widely in AKC field trials, as well as in bench shows, leading to highly refined development of the breed.

It is an interesting fact that the Beagle has gone on to be more popular in the U.S. and Canada than in their native country. It has ranked in the top 10 most popular breeds for over 30 years and even held the number one spot from 1953 to 1959 on the list of the American Kennel Club's registered breeds, and consistently remains in the top 5 each year.

Beagle Field Trials

In the U.K., hunting is now banned, and even trail/drag hunting is unpopular. The sport of Beagle field trials is only found in the United States and Canada. Until the 1980s, packs of Beagles competed as a unit or team, but increasingly the interest of enthusiasts focused on the development of the trailing abilities of individual hounds called "singles."

As available open land dwindled in the face of industrialization, Beagle clubs were forced to acquire and rehabilitate land and to become "rabbit farmers" to keep their sport alive. Today there are more than 525 Beagle clubs in the United States, each in possession of 150 acres or more of land.

Once the native rabbits were confined to fenced lands, they changed their habits, and dogs in America were selectively bred to be meticulous and slow tracking specialists. Like their ancestors in England, American Beagles developed in close relationship to the animals they chased.

Today there are four types of Beagle field trials:

- Brace — Pairs of hounds compete by gender in pursuit of the cottontail rabbit.

- Gun Dog Brace — The dogs are cast to search and tested for gun shyness.

- Small Pack — Packs of 4–7 hounds run in competition and are later tested for gun-shyness.

- Large Pack — Held in northern states where the snowshoe hare is found, these trials involve packs of 30–60 hounds.

Beagle Breed Characteristics

Although Beagles adapt well to life indoors, they need early socialization, especially if they will be living in a home with other pets. Because they are scent dogs, they must be kept on the leash during outings if you don't want them to take off chasing a "trail." There is a tendency toward being stubborn, so prepare yourself to firmly establish your position as leader of the pack.

We asked **Cindy Williams of Honey Pot Hounds** what makes the Beagle so special: "The Beagle is a wonderful breed for many reasons but mostly I think their temperament and personality are what keep

Photo Credit: Cindy Williams of Honey Pot Hounds.

people coming back to these little hounds. A Beagle will always be loving and sweet, but Beagles are certainly not always obedient and they are almost never boring. A Beagle will keep himself busy literally nosing into whatever he can, always searching and seeking to find some tasty morsel, toy to play with (or destroy!) or critter to chase. This 'busybodiness' can be both cute and comical but also annoying and dangerous, and a Beagle needs a responsible owner and a safe environment if he is to stay out of trouble while following his innate passion for nosiness.

"Another advantage that the Beagle has over many of the other breeds of dog is his medium size and short coat. The Beagle is a perfect size to fit on your lap and isn't too big for most children to safely play with.

Many older children and adults can pick up the Beagle which has its advantages, especially when doing one of those oh so typical Beagle owner activities like retrieving them from the kitchen trashcan."

Physical Size and Appearance

Beagles closely resemble their larger relative the Foxhound, but if the two dogs were standing side by side, it would be clear that the Beagle has a broader head and shorter muzzle (nose and mouth).

Beagles come in two size varieties in the U.S.: up to 13 inches, and over 13 inches but not to exceed 15 inches. In the U.K., Australia and Europe, the U.K. standard is used with desirable height range being 13–16 inches.

Know from the beginning of your relationship with this breed that **obesity is a serious problem** with Beagles, demanding proper management of their nutrition and a strict policy about "treats."

Expect their fully grown weight to be approximately 22 to 30 pounds (9.97 to 13.60 kg) for a 13" Beagle. For a 13" to 15" Beagle, average weight is from 25 to 35 pounds (11.33 to 15.87 kg).

Ruth Darlene Stewart of Aladar Beagles: "The American Kennel Club does not recognize a 'Pocket Beagle.' This term is used by breeders that are uninformed about the breed or trying to charge extra money for abnormally small puppies.

"The variety of the Beagle, 13 or 15 inches, is decided by the height of the dog at the shoulders (withers) at maturity. Any Beagle 13 inches or under at maturity is called a 13. Even if it is 12 inches tall, it is still a 13" Beagle in classification. A Beagle that is 14 inches or 13 1/2 inches at the shoulder is called a 15-inch Beagle. Any Beagle over 15 inches at the shoulder is disqualified from AKC Conformation events.

"It is almost impossible to accurately predict the size a puppy will be as an adult when the puppy is only 8–12 weeks old. Reputable breeders keep statistics of their puppies and can make an educated guess between 8–12 weeks of age, but we have all had those puppies that surprised us and grew larger than we thought or stayed a 13. Thirteen-inch males are hard to get and anyone wanting a 13-inch male or female should plan on being on a waiting list."

On average, an adult Beagle stands 13–16 inches / 33–41 cm at the withers and weighs 18–35 lbs. / 8.2–15.9 kg. Females are slightly smaller at 12–14 inches / 33–38 cm.

The dog's skull should be domed with a smooth line over a medium and square muzzle. The nose is generally black and has a "gumdrop" shape. The strong jawline accentuates the noble profile, softened toward the body by the soft droop of the low set, long ears with their lovely rounded tips.

Beagles look out at the world with large, mild eyes of brown or hazel. Their expression is well-suited for the breed's tendency to beg for treats and whatever is on your plate.

When a Beagle is of a proper weight, they have a medium length, strong neck, and a broad chest that narrows toward a tapered waist at the abdomen. The tail, which is tipped in white, should be carried gaily with a slight curve and should have the characteristic "brush."

Overall, this is a muscular little dog that stands on straight front legs and stronger rear legs with a pronounced bend at the stifle. The Beagle looks like what he is, a little hound ready for athletic action.

Bev Davies-Fraser of Waskasoo Kennel: "Anything over 15" is a disqualification in Beagles in North America. Judges are provided with metal wickets to measure any Beagle they feel may not meet the height restrictions. Another difference is body type. In North America you tend to see a much shorter back giving the impression that the Beagle is square. While this issue is a hot button topic in North America, the consensus is that the U.K. Beagle is too long in back to meet the AKC standard. Because of the past quarantine situation in the U.K., there were not many North American types imported to the U.K. Visually, you can tell the difference in both Beagles. In the last decade or so, Americans and Canadians have been importing more lines from Europe, Scandinavia, and Australia, as well as the U.K. As a result of that, we are seeing more Beagles that are less square and consequently better movers. We are always trying to improve structure and movement. The North American Standard does not address movement, but it is still something that all breeders strive to improve upon. The U.S. standard is fairly subjective so breeders are always discussing their interpretation of the standard and how it applies to the Beagles we see in the ring today.

"Beagles are very popular in Canada. However, show Beagles are in the minority compared to field-bred. Eastern Canada has many field trials and most field-bred Beagles come from Ontario and Manitoba. West of Manitoba we do not have any field competitions. Show breeders in Canada are but a handful compared to the U.S. I will say, however, that the quality of the Canadian Beagle can go up against an American Beagle at any time. In fact, the 2015 Westminster Best in Show winner was a Beagle bred in Canada, affectionately known as 'Miss P.'

The Exceptional Nose

The three breeds with the most highly regarded sense of smell are the Bloodhound, Basset Hound, and the Beagle. In a study conducted in the 1950s, a Beagle was able to locate a mouse in a one-acre field in less than a minute. As a basis for comparison, a Fox Terrier needed 15 minutes and a Scottish Terrier failed the test completely.

Beagles are at their best when following a trail on the ground. For this reason, they are not typically chosen for rescue work like other breeds, such as the Collie, that have superior air-scenting capabilities. Beagles are, however, excellent at other kinds of scent work.

The U.S. Department of Agriculture, for instance, employs Beagles in its Animal and Plant Health Inspection Service to locate contraband items including food in airports. Beagles used by the service have a 90% accuracy rating and can detect as many as 50 distinct odors.

Popular Coats and Colors

The Beagle has a smooth double coat well-suited to wet weather. When kept as pets, they should be brushed once a week. They do shed, but not to excess, and the hairs are very short. The breed does not require frequent bathing. Due to the limited amount of air circulation under the ear flap, they can be prone to ear infection. Preventive ear cleaning is recommended.

Sam Goldberg of BeagleHealth.info: "Beagles have a good weatherproof coat and although short, it is dense and will shed rain. They do shed and it can be surprising how much hair one Beagle can produce!"

Tricolor Beagles

The most common coloration seen in Beagles is the classic tricolor — solid patches of tan and white with a black saddle called the "blackback" or "black blanketed." It is also possible for a tricolor dog to have faint brown markings inside the black to create the "Dark Tri" coat. A lighter version is called the "Faded Tri."

It is important to stress that just because the traditional tricolor is most popular it doesn't make a Beagle with a different coloring any better or worse — all Beagles are equals.

Tricolor Beagles are not born this way; initially they are black and white. The white areas are set by age eight weeks, but the black areas can sometimes fade to brown as they get older or even disappear altogether.

Sam Goldberg of BeagleHealth.info: "The tricolor can also come in a 'broken' version where there are much larger

Photo Credit: Carol and Lori Norman of Lokavi Beagles.

white patches breaking up the saddle pattern. Although often described as English type, these can be found in other countries and some breeders favour them as brightly marked.

"The black can be modified by the dilution gene to produce a blue instead of the black, or a brown gene to produce a liver colour instead of black. This is combined with the tan and white to produce the blue/tan and white or liver/tan and white."

Two-color

Sam Goldberg of BeagleHealth.info: "This is a white with one other colour — lemon, tan, or red — and these are just depths of shades of the same gene. In Beagles we don't have brown or liver on white. Technically according to the Kennel Club it is supposed to be possible to have a black and white Beagle but no one has recorded one."

Pied Beagles

Found less frequently than the types already discussed are pied Beagles where they display broken markings (In the U.S., this is more commonly called an open-marked Beagle).

In other words, the three basic colors of tan, white, and black intermingle and do not occur in solid patches (except for white).

In areas where the hairs of one color dominate, this changes the look and these shades of color have specific names. "Lemon Pied" is a Beagle with mostly lemon or cream hairs intermingled with black and white. "Hare Pied" is mostly tan then black, and "Badger Pied" is mostly black hairs.

Mottles/Ticking

You may also see the word ticking, flecks, or (in the U.K.) mottle. This is a separate color pattern and can overlay the white on any other hound color. Thus you can have a tan and white with small black and tan spots on the white parts. These spots can also occur on the white parts on a tricolor.

The mottle gene is inherited separately from the white patterning and that is separate again from the color expression gene, which gives tricolor or bicolor in various shades.

Bev Davies-Fraser of Waskasoo Kennel: "There are also diluted colours. Blue is a dilute for the blacks, and lilac is the dilute for the liver colour. Liver is an accepted colour in the U.S., but not in the U.K."

Ruth Darlene Stewart of Aladar Beagles: "Beagles come in any hound color with the black, white, and tan or tri-color Beagles being the common, and the red and white being the second-most frequently seen.

"Other hound colors such as blues or chocolates (liver) also are accepted colors, although these colors are not shown as often, as they usually correlate to a light-colored eye. This simple fact of a light-colored eye may be enough to eliminate a puppy as a show/breeding potential for some breeders.

"There are breeders that advertise RARE or NEW Beagle colors and use 'DESIGNER' type names for the colors shown on the NBC site. These are not rare colors. Norwegian Blue and Russian Blue are 'new' colors that have appeared over the last few years. These colors are actually the expression of the Merle gene. Experts have stated in the past that this dominant gene did not exist in the Beagle population. Most reputable breeders may use the recessive colors in their breeding program, if the overall quality of the dog is excellent. But REPUTABLE breeders do not breed for color alone!!"

We asked **Carol and Lori Norman of Lokavi Beagles** about the suitability of Beagles for people with allergies: "Beagles are not hypoallergenic, and a person with allergies may have issues. As always, I answer generically, as not all dogs have the same coat (and all people with allergies don't have the same degree), but most Beagles do have an undercoat that sheds. Although it is a fault in the breed, a Beagle with a 'seal' coat (has only top guard hair, flat to the skin, with no undercoat) would probably be better for someone with allergies. However, you don't know that as a young puppy, and they will still shed. If someone has a general allergy to dogs, then a Beagle is normally not a good choice."

What to Expect — The Beagle Puppy

Bringing a new puppy home is fun, even if the memories you're making include epic, puppy-generated messes! Young dogs are a huge responsibility no matter how much you love them, and they take a lot of work.

Beagle puppies **can be stubborn**. They are bred to be pack animals, so you must show them early on that you are the "leader." Like all young dogs, they need early socialization, and they must not be encouraged to bark or howl. While it's impossible to get a Beagle to be completely quiet, you can teach him to stop making noise on command.

The first few weeks with any dog is an important phase that shapes the animal's adult behavior and temperament. Every new pet owner hopes to have a well-mannered, obedient, and happy companion.

As scent hounds, Beagles must be kept leashed, so good etiquette while on the lead is an important early lesson. The breed is not good about coming when called, and they really can't be left alone outside. They'll dig, climb, and howl when they get bored.

Sam Goldberg of BeagleHealth.info adds: "Beagles are bred to think for themselves when hunting to work a scent. They appear stubborn and you need to be more interesting than whatever has taken their fancy."

Thanks to a copious appetite, Beagles may dig in the trash and steal food from the table. Do not let these behaviors get started in puppyhood, or you'll find it very difficult to change your stubborn dog's mind!

If you don't have the time to spend working with your Beagle in the areas that will make him a desirable companion, ask yourself if this is really the time in your life to have a pet. What is your work schedule? Do you have to travel often and for extended periods? Only purchase a Beagle if you have time to spend with him.

Initially **you will need to devote several hours a day** to your new puppy. You have to housetrain and feed him every day, giving him your attention and starting to slowly introduce the house rules, as well as take care of his general health and welfare. Remember too that treating Beagles like babies is something many owners succumb to and this is not at all good for them.

Certainly for the first few days (ideally two weeks), one of your family should be **around at all times of the day** to help him settle and to start bonding with him. The last thing you should do is buy a puppy and leave him alone in the house after just a day or two. They will feel isolated, bored, and sad, and this leads to behavioral problems.

As well as time, there is a financial cost, not just the initial cost of your puppy. You also have to be prepared to spend money on regular healthcare, potential emergency money in vet bills in the case of illness, as well as equipment such as crates, bedding, and toys.

Photo Credit: Ruth Darlene Stewart of Aladar Beagles.

DID YOU KNOW? Research shows many dogs have intelligence and understanding levels similar to a two-year-old child. They can understand around 150 words and **can solve problems**, as well as devise tricks to play on people and other animals.

Personality and Temperament

So what defines your Beagle's character? One factor is his **temperament**, which is an inherited trait, and another factor is the **environment** in which your Beagle grows up. In a dog's life, the first few months are deemed really important. When the time comes that he becomes separated from the litter, his reactions and responses to the world around him are a reflection of how he has learned the essence of socialization.

There is no denying the **benefits** that your Beagle gets from being introduced early to other dogs and humans along with different noises and smells. When a dog learns how to feel comfortable in whatever type of surrounding he is in, feelings of fear and anxiety can be eliminated. Otherwise these feelings can cause a dog to display undesirable behavior such as aggression.

Apart from their famous "selective deafness" when it comes to being called or trained to do something they don't want to do, Beagles are **friendly** by nature, peaceful with other pets in the house, and **good** with children.

Beagles are very **intelligent and loyal**. Although small in size, they are brave and devoted, alerting their owners to anything they perceive to be a danger. If there is one thing a Beagle can do well, it's making noise. They may not be guard dogs, but they are excellent watch dogs. You will always know when someone is in the vicinity of your property.

To get around problem behaviors that are an expression of boredom or separation anxiety, you must ensure that your dog gets plenty of exercise. Beagles are easily distracted, especially by scents, and very curious. Establish yourself as the alpha in the "pack" to keep your dog directed. All dogs respond well to consistency and repetition.

Regardless of your authority, however, a Beagle on the "trail" **ignores everything** in pursuit of his quarry. This breed must stay leashed at all times when outside for their own safety. Left unattended in a fenced yard a Beagle will promptly dig out to go "exploring."

Beagles do well with crate training. Getting your dog accustomed to the crate as quickly as possible will cut down on the number of messes you're cleaning up in the first few weeks.

Lindsay Bryson of Allegro Beagles: "The Beagle is known for their independence and stubborn personalities. This is a breed that loves to think on their own and will often outsmart their owners. They enjoy problem solving and if there is something they want, they will go for it, despite what the repercussions may be. They love people and other animals and should always have a merry attitude in everything they do. A shy or aloof personality is not typical. The most important thing to remember about the Beagle is once their nose turns on, their ears turn off and it will be hard to call them off the scent. This is why it is important to never trust a Beagle off leash."

Joan Wurst of Everwind Beagles: "The Beagle is an energetic dog with an outgoing disposition. They are kind, gentle, even-tempered, and very friendly, thus they make wonderful family pets that can be trusted with children. They love everyone and expect everyone to love them."

Can the Beagle Co-exist with Other Pets?

Beagles tend to be quite peaceful with other dogs, especially if they have been raised with their housemates. You need to be **very careful** having a hunting dog around rabbits, hamsters, ferrets, and other small creatures that will look like something to be chased, although breeders such as Susie Arden have had positive experiences (see her comment).

I would not completely rule out having a Beagle in a household where a cat is already established, and the Beagle enters the picture as a puppy. Cats have a way of putting young dogs firmly in their place, and Beagles do respond strongly to perceived "pack" order.

Peter and Val Davies of Barrvale Beagles: "In my experience there is not (usually) a problem relating to cats. They will sometimes even share baskets. I even know of a Beagle who has a hamster chum!"

Sandra Groeschel of The Whim says: "Beagles do very well with other dogs. In regard to other types of pets, it depends. One needs to remember that Beagles are basically hunting dogs (rabbits in particular). I would be especially cautious attempting to bring an adult Beagle into an environment with other pets and would closely monitor the Beagle's behavior to ensure everyone's safety. One might be more successful at having a co-existing collection of pets if the Beagle is raised from puppyhood around the other pets. In any case, all the pets should be watched over to avoid any problems."

Susie Arden of Madika Beagles: "Beagles living happily alongside cats is actually quite common. They seemed to know that the cats rule and typically the cat makes sure the Beagles are kept in their place, below them.

Photo Credit: Susie Arden of Madika Beagles. This is Emma and her daughter Dottie with long haired Syrian hamster Norman, Dottie's much-loved pet.

"Small critters are something else. Every Beagle owner has said their Beagle would kill the hamster, yet ALL my Beagles live happily with hamsters, rats, and degus.

"It all began when I was given Wee Ham (the hamster), as he couldn't be handled by his owner. Miles — U.K. Ch. Madika Nut Case — was instantly smitten and clearly loved the little guy so much so that when Wee Ham died, Miles was quite distraught and after two weeks of watching him search for his little friend, we bought him another hamster!!

"Next came the family of degus, then the rats, all of which Miles adored. Interestingly all three Beagles were adults when the critters arrived. Miles was immediately interested in them yet so gentle, licking and nuzzling them despite being an excellent hunting dog.

"You've got to know your dog extremely well to be able to trust it not to kill it even if by accident. I also found the little furries show no fear towards the Beagles and their boldness certainly helps."

Is the Beagle Safe with Children?

Beagles have high energy levels that make them good dogs for children. They are active, sometimes to the point of being "hyper," but since the breed needs a lot of exercise, it's actually good for the dog to play with the kids until both sides of the equation drop from exhaustion. Beagles love the activity, and they can have a fun and entertaining sense of humor chasing balls and engaging in games.

As is true for any dog, it is important that you supervise any interaction between your children and the dog. Young children may not understand that a small dog like the Beagle is fragile and they might unknowingly hurt the dog or treat it too roughly. You are unlikely to have any trouble with your Beagle interacting with children, but all dogs have the capacity to become aggressive if they are frightened or mistreated. Teach your children how to properly handle a dog, especially when it is still a puppy, to prevent incidents.

Photo Credit: Veronica and Rosie Longman of Chatoyant Beagles.

Don't tolerate rough or aggressive play from either, and explain to children that Beagles like "nice touches." When puppies get too rough or mouth their fingers when teething, respond with a firm, "No!" Soon enough, all parties will get the point.

Even if you do not have children, it is advisable to expose your dog to children during puppyhood to prepare the animal to behave correctly during any future encounters. Being good around children is a critical part of any well-behaved dog's repertoire of manners.

For prospective owners with young children, I'd encourage them to select a puppy from a breeder who has socialized their dogs with children of all ages. This helps to make sure the puppy is confident enough around children to tolerate their odd sounds and movements. Temperament is key — a shy, reserved, or anxious puppy should never be considered for a home with children. When a puppy lives in a home with children, it is important to have a crate or other safe space for the puppy to retreat to when the kids become too much!

Veronica and Rosie Longman of Chatoyant Beagles: "Puppies and small children are hard work and time consuming, so it usually best to encourage prospective owners to wait until children are around school age before buying a Beagle puppy."

Ann Roth of Hounds of Harnett says: "Well-bred Beagles make excellent family pets for the right homes. They are very patient and tolerant with children. However, the adults in the household need to supervise and make sure the children don't overfeed the dog or leave a gate or door open so the Beagle can escape. These loving hounds have been bred as independent hunters for generations, and can be quite stubborn when on a scent, so absolutely must be kept in a securely fenced area or on lead at all times."

Edy Ballard of Ironwood Beagles: "While it's true that Beagles are 'sturdy' hounds, any puppy can be injured or frightened by the unintentional rough handling by a toddler. Any breed of dog will nip or bite if teased, mishandled, or hurt by a young child. Very young children and puppies should always be supervised closely. When supervised properly, Beagles can be one of the best breeds for a child to grow up with and will be buddies for life."

Sam Goldberg of BeagleHealth.info: "Beagles do make very good family pets, but they are sensitive, and children need to understand any dog needs space at times. Here is where an indoor kennel or crate can be made into a den for the new addition to retire to for some peace and quiet. All children should be taught that every dog needs time alone sometimes."

Is Male or Female Preferable?

Typically my position on gender is that **it doesn't matter**. Concentrate instead on the **personality** of the individual dog. This line of thinking seems to hold true for Beagles, with no discernible difference in the temperament of females over males.

The only time gender is important is if you are intending to breed the dog. Otherwise, focus on the individual Beagle's personality. In too many instances, people want female puppies because they assume they will be sweeter and gentler. No valid basis exists for this assumption. The real determining factor in any dog's long-term behavior is the quality of its training in relation to its place in the family. Consistency in addressing bad behaviors before they start is crucial.

Female dogs coddled as puppies display more negative behavior and

greater territoriality than males. Consider this factor with a grown Beagle, especially in a rescue situation. A Beagle's temperament needs to match the household to which it is going. So many owners want female puppies, but in many situations a neutered male is a much better fit.

When it comes to dogs like the Beagle, there are few physical distinctions between the sexes. The only difference you are likely to notice between a male and female Beagle is that the female might be a little smaller than the male.

Photo Credit: Natasha Bell of Alfadais Beagles.

In terms of behavior, sometimes male Beagles mature a little more slowly than females, so you might notice more puppy-like behavior from a male Beagle puppy than a female once they reach 8 to 10 months of age. This might affect training – female Beagles that develop faster than males become mature sooner and will likely respond to training better. Male Beagles that are neutered tend to be less dominant than non-neutered male dogs – they may also be less likely to develop problem behaviors.

In general, you should spay or neuter your dog if you do not plan to breed it (but this is **not recommended** before the age of 12 months). Breeding your Beagle is not a decision that you should make lightly, and it is definitely not something you should do if your only reason is to make a profit.

To find subtle differences between the genders, I look to "pack behavior" in the wild. Females will focus on only one male in terms of breeding. Males will focus on all females available for breeding. This can result in females sometimes having a special fondness for one member of the family. Males do not. Having said this, the influence is so slight in a human family one may not notice this, especially if all members of the family give the puppy lots of attention and interaction. I tell families that if they have a situation where one member of the family is gone all week, coming home on weekends only, they may want to consider a male who won't really "notice" this absence during the week.

Peter and Val Davies of Barrvale Beagles share their opinions: "When deciding which is best for your family, a female or a male, it is a very easy decision. There are really no real differences in temperament or trainability. Beagles are individuals, like people, some are brighter than others, some more stubborn than others, some more idle than others. It is nothing to do with male/female. Both sexes are equally affectionate, love-me-do dogs and are always willing to play, joining in with family life. Regarding trainability, again no real difference and they will learn anything for a tit-bit being real foodies and very intelligent.

"The only reason for choosing a female over a male is size, and that is not hard and fast, as some males are not as big as some females. The breed standard allows for the possibility of a 13-inch male and a 16-inch female. That aside, I feel an elderly person may be better with a female, as they are, generally speaking, smaller and less strong than a male and so easier to cope with. A boy could get very heavy on your knee after a while. This could also apply to a family with very young children."

Chapter 2 — The Beagle Breed Standard

The breed standard provides the main blueprint for a number of dog attributes that include a dog breed's physical appearance, his unique moves, and the type of temperament that each breed is expected to have. Created and laid down by the breed societies, dogs that are purebred (pedigree) have their registrations kept by the American Kennel Club (AKC) and the Kennel Club (in the U.K.).

http://www.akc.org/
https://www.thekennelclub.org.uk/

Breeders approved by the Kennel Clubs have consented to breed puppies based on strict standards of breeding. They do not just simply mate any available male or female (sire or dam).

The following standard was approved by the American Kennel Club in 1957 and differs only slightly from The Kennel Club standard used in the U.K. It is reproduced verbatim here for reference purposes. The only changes incorporated are typographical to enhance readability.

AKC Official Standard for the Beagle

Head:

The skull should be fairly long, slightly domed at occiput, with cranium broad and full.

Ears — Ears set on moderately low, long, reaching when drawn out nearly, if not quite, to the end of the nose; fine in texture, fairly broad, with almost entire absence of erectile power-setting close to the head, with the forward edge slightly inturning to the cheek-rounded at tip.

Eyes — Eyes large, set well apart; soft and houndlike-expression gentle and pleading; of a brown or hazel color.

Muzzle — Muzzle of medium length; straight and square-cut; the stop moderately defined.

Jaws — Level. Lips free from flews; nostrils large and open.

Defects — A very flat skull, narrow across the top; excess of dome, eyes small, sharp and terrierlike, or prominent and protruding; muzzle long, snipy or cut away decidedly below the eyes, or very short. Roman-nosed, or upturned, giving a dish-face expression. Ears short, set on high or with a tendency to rise above the point of origin.

Body:

Neck and Throat — Neck rising free and light from the shoulders, strong in substance yet not loaded, of medium length. The throat clean and free from folds of skin; a slight wrinkle below the angle of the jaw, however, may be allowable.

Defects — A thick, short, cloddy neck carried on a line with the top of the shoulders. Throat showing dewlap and folds of skin to a degree termed "throatiness."

Shoulders and Chest:

Shoulders sloping — clean, muscular, not heavy or loaded; conveying the idea of freedom of action with activity and strength. Chest deep and broad, but not broad enough to interfere with the free play of the shoulders.

Defects — Straight, upright shoulders. Chest disproportionately wide or with lack of depth.

Back, Loin and Ribs:

Back short, muscular and strong. Loin broad and slightly arched, and the ribs well sprung, giving abundance of lung room.

Defects — Very long or swayed or roached back. Flat, narrow loin. Flat ribs.

Forelegs and Feet:

Forelegs — Straight, with plenty of bone in proportion to size of the hound. Pasterns short and straight.

Feet — Close, round and firm. Pad full and hard.

Defects — Out at elbows. Knees knuckled over forward, or bent backward. Forelegs crooked or Dachshundlike. Feet long, open or spreading.

Hips, Thighs, Hind Legs and Feet:

Hips and thighs strong and well-muscled, giving abundance of propelling power. Stifles strong and well let down. Hocks firm, symmetrical and moderately bent. Feet close and firm.

Defects — Cowhocks, or straight hocks. Lack of muscle and propelling power. Open feet.

Tail:

Set moderately high; carried gaily, but not turned forward over the back; with slight curve; short as compared with size of the hound; with brush.

Defects — A long tail. Teapot curve or inclined forward from the root. Rat tail with absence of brush.

Coat:

A close, hard, hound coat of medium length.

Defects — A short, thin coat, or of a soft quality.

Color:

Any true hound color.

General Appearance:

A miniature Foxhound, solid and big for his inches, with the wear-and-tear look of the hound that can last in the chase and follow his quarry to the death.

Varieties:

There shall be two varieties: Thirteen Inch, which shall be for hounds not exceeding 13 inches in height; Fifteen Inch, which shall be for hounds over 13 but not exceeding 15 inches in height.

Disqualification: Any hound measuring more than 15 inches shall be disqualified.

U.K. Kennel Club Official Standard for the Beagle

Last updated January 2010

General Appearance

A sturdy, compactly built hound, conveying the impression of quality without coarseness.

Characteristics

A merry hound whose essential function is to hunt, primarily hare, by following a scent. Bold, with great activity, stamina and determination. Alert, intelligent and of even temperament.

Temperament

Amiable and alert, showing no aggression or timidity.

Head and Skull

Fair length, powerful without being coarse, finer in the bitch, free from frown and wrinkle. Skull slightly domed, moderately wide, with slight peak. Stop well defined and dividing length, between occiput and tip of nose, as equally as possible. Muzzle not snipy, lips reasonably well flewed. Nose broad, preferably black, but less pigmentation permissible in lighter coloured hounds. Nostrils wide.

Eyes

Dark brown or hazel, fairly large, not deep set or prominent, set well apart with mild, appealing expression.

Ears

Long, with rounded tip, reaching nearly to end of nose when drawn out. Set on low, fine in texture and hanging gracefully close to cheeks.

Mouth

The jaws should be strong, with a perfect, regular and complete scissor bite, i.e., upper teeth closely overlapping lower teeth and set square to the jaws.

Neck

Sufficiently long to enable hound to come down easily to scent, slightly arched and showing little dewlap.

Forequarters

Shoulders well laid back, not loaded. Forelegs straight and upright well under the hound, good substance, and round in bone, not tapering off to feet. Pasterns short. Elbows firm, turning neither in nor out. Height to elbow about half height at withers.

Body

Topline straight and level. Chest let down to below elbow. Ribs well sprung and extending well back. Short in the couplings but well balanced. Loins powerful and supple, without excessive tuck-up.

Hindquarters

Muscular thighs. Stifles well bent. Hocks firm, well let down and parallel to each other.

Feet

Tight and firm. Well knuckled up and strongly padded. Not hare-footed. Nails short.

Tail

Sturdy, moderately long. Set on high, carried gaily but not curled over back or inclined forward from root. Well covered with hair, especially on underside.

Gait/Movement

Back level, firm with no indication of roll. Stride free, long-reaching in front and straight without high action; hindlegs showing drive. Should not move close behind nor paddle nor plait in front.

Coat

Short, dense and weatherproof.

Colour

Tricolour (black, tan and white); blue, white and tan; badger pied; hare pied; lemon pied; lemon and white; red and white; tan and white; black and white; all white. With the exception of all white, all the above mentioned colours can be found as mottle. No other colours are permissible. Tip of stern white.

Size

Desirable minimum height at withers: 33 cms (13 ins). Desirable maximum height at withers: 40 cms (16 ins).

Faults

Any departure from the foregoing points should be considered a fault and the seriousness with which the fault should be regarded should be in exact proportion to its degree and its effect upon the health and welfare of the dog and on the dog's ability to perform its traditional work.

Note: Male animals should have two apparently normal testicles fully descended into the scrotum.

Chapter 3 — Is the Beagle the Right Dog?

Beagle "people" need to be patient, loving, flexible dog owners who are committed to training their pets and creating an environment for them that supports their wellbeing, their best behavior, and gives them emotional security.

You also must understand that you could be signing on for a 10–15-year (or more) relationship with an intelligent and fairly demanding little dog. Understand from the beginning that your Beagle will not settle down and become an adult emotionally for 12–18 months.

Many owners give up on their Beagles during this crucial period of life, choosing instead to give the dogs away or to abandon them at shelters.

Think about what's going on in your own life. Don't purchase a dog at a time when you have a huge commitment at work or there's a lot of disruption. Dogs, especially very smart ones like Beagles, **thrive on routine**. You want adequate time to bond with your pet, and to help the little dog understand how his new world "runs."

As a small, compact hound, the Beagle has a lot going for him. He's handsome, easy to groom, peaceful with other dogs, and friendly with people while remaining a good watch dog. The major thing you have to understand, however, is that no matter how cute a Beagle is when he gazes up at you with those soulful eyes, **he is still a hunting dog**, and he interacts with the world based on that hardwiring.

Beagles need a lot of exercise and most don't get enough, which is why obesity is such a problem with the breed. They can live in apartments, but only if they are exercised daily. They must be kept leashed, and if turned loose in a fenced yard, they have to be watched. He can dig his way under a fence before you've had time to close the back door. They're also phenomenal at climbing over what they can't get under.

On the one hand, these dogs are single-minded in their independent determination to do things their way, but can be easily distracted by a scent. Both of these inherent qualities mean obedience training is not optional. **It's a necessity**.

Beagles can be neurotic, aggressive, or fearful (just like any other dog) if they have come from the wrong background and not been nurtured properly. The only way to avoid getting a dog with these issues is to work with a reputable breeder that has a well-developed breeding program. Although dogs from such establishments are typically more expensive, the extra cost is more than worth it in the long run.

Sam Goldberg of BeagleHealth.info: "I would say from experience as a vet that Beagles fall in this category far less than many breeds, particularly the small designer breeds."

We asked some of our contributing breeders some questions to help you decide if the Beagle is the right dog for you.

Is the Beagle suitable for a person or family that works all day?

Gary Clacher of Misken Beagles is emphatic: "Absolutely NO! They are pack animals — just as cows are herd animals … you never see one cow on its own in a field."

Veronica and Rosie Longman of Chatoyant Beagles: "NO dog should be left all day."

Is the Beagle breed suitable for a first-time dog owner?

Alayne Rae Mullen of Lane Rae Beagles: "Beagles are an outstanding breed selection for first time and experienced dog owners. Though selecting a puppy with the correct energy level and train-ability is most important to ensure correct placement, Beagles have a very gentle disposition and easily form a life-long bond with their family members. Depending on the individual puppy, they are very well suited for a very active family or more laid back individual and can thrive in many situations, as long as they are provided with an adequate amount of exercise and training. The Beagle is a very smart breed and caution should be taken to ensure your Beagle is not able to access counter tops, food bins and escape enclosed areas. They do best with a very strict schedule right from the start, as well as early socialization and training. I would recommend this 'Merry Hound' to anyone looking for a smaller breed that requires little grooming as an exceptional family companion or competition prospect."

Does the Beagle make for a good guard dog?

Gary Clacher of Misken Beagles: "A Beagle does make a good watch dog in my opinion, as they are, by nature, both curious and 'singers.' Mine will sit on top of the sofa and watch for any and all movement outside and then run round the back of the house to come to the front fence and 'greet.' If anyone was stupid enough to break into my house I'd certainly know about it very quickly (although any intruder is more at risk of ultimately being licked to death rather than savaged!)"

Carol and Lori Norman of Lokavi Beagles: "Beagles are a breed that will bark when a stranger comes to the door, but they are not going to go any further towards keeping them out. Beagles have a reputation for barking, but to what degree starts with whether your pup comes from field or show lines. There is a tremendous difference. Dogs bred for hunting are bred to have a big 'bay,' or bark ... it is what the hunters strive for. Hunters must follow these dogs through the field and the voice on a Beagle tells them where the dogs are moving, and if they are on a scent.

"Beagles bred from show lines are bred to be companions, and performance (Obedience, Agility, Rally, etc.) dogs. They are usually not good hunters, and usually don't have the big Beagle 'bay.' They much prefer staying with the family, and not getting up early to go walk on the prickly grass.

"Beagles are social dogs, and with a pack dog mentality, wants to be with someone. A show-bred Beagle pup will bark if left alone too often. They want to be integrated into the family so love to go on hikes, trips, camping, boating, etc. They don't like to be alone. A field-bred Beagle will want to hunt, and they bark for the pure joy of it. They have a wonderful temperament and love people, but they want to hunt something … it is what they were bred to do. Your neighbors will know he is there."

Can the Beagle be described as greedy and prone to weight issues?

Carol and Lori Norman of Lokavi Beagles: "YES! Beagles do tend to get fat. You definitely must watch how much you feed them … including how many treats they get and whether you feed scraps from the table. They will stare you down with those pleading eyes, and steal what you leave unattended. Don't give in! An overweight dog, like with people, will cause health problems. Learn to avoid the stare, and make sure you don't leave food where they can reach it.

"If you are afraid your dog is not getting enough to eat, in preparing the full portion meal, mix a half-portion of your dog food and a half-portion size canned, unsalted, green beans. Green beans will act as a filler, but won't cause weight gain. Never feed green beans alone, as they will not receive proper nutrition. Also, instead of giving them a full treat, give them half a treat … they don't measure! This will cut their food in half without them starving."

Do I Need a License?

Some countries have strict licensing requirements for the keeping of particular animals. Even if you are not legally required to have a license for your Beagle, you might still want to consider getting one. Having a license means that there is an official record of your ownership so, should someone find your dog when he gets lost, that person will be able to find your contact information and reconnect you with him.

Although there are no federal regulations in the United States regarding the licensing of dogs, most states do require that dogs be licensed by their owners, otherwise you may be subject to a fine. Fortunately, dog licenses are inexpensive (usually around $25) and fairly easy to obtain — you simply file an application with the state and then renew the license each year.

Edy Ballard of Ironwood Beagles: "Most states do require that dogs be licensed by their owners. However, in the U.S. most dog licensing laws are local ordinances, usually by county, not state. Many municipalities (such as in rural areas) don't require dog licensing at all. Prospective owners should check with their county or city to find out what is required. A rabies vaccine is almost always required by law."

No license is needed to own a dog in the U.K., although it is mandatory to microchip all dogs over 8 weeks, so any Beagle you buy or adopt must already be chipped. It is also a legal requirement in the U.K. for any dog to wear a collar and tag in a public place.

Puppy or Adult Beagle?

After you decide that you want a Beagle, you still have an important decision to make — do you want to purchase a puppy or an adult dog? There are pros and cons to each side of the issue, so you should think carefully before you make your decision.

People love puppies for all the obvious reasons. They are adorable, and the younger the dog when you buy him, the longer your time with your pet. At an average **lifespan prediction of 10–15 years**, Beagles are long-lived in relation to their size.

When you purchase a Beagle puppy, you get to raise the puppy in whatever way you like — you have the power to influence his temperament through socialization, and you can also train him as you like. A downside to puppies is that their personalities may change as they grow and develop — picking a puppy based on personality may backfire because the adult dog could be very different from the puppy.

While raising a Beagle puppy can be fun and exciting, it is also very challenging. If you purchase a puppy, you will have to deal with things like teething, potty training, and obedience training. Puppies tend to get into mischief, so you might have to deal with problem behaviors like chewing or whining.

Buying or adopting an adult Beagle will not necessarily spare you from all of these challenges, but the dog will probably already be housebroken and might have some training under its belt.

Photo Credit: Gary Clacher of Misken Beagles.

When you do take in a rescue dog, find out as much as possible about the dog's background and the **reason for its surrender**. Beagles are often given up for issues with digging, barking, and aggression toward other dogs. If these problems are a consequence of environment or treatment, however, it may be possible to correct them. Additionally, pets living with the elderly are frequently surrendered when their owner dies or goes into a care facility but are perfectly well-behaved.

Adopting an adult dog is a good idea because there are millions of homeless pets living in animal shelters, so adopting an adult dog rather than buying a puppy will help to reduce the unwanted pet population.

In adopting a Beagle you **could also be saving the dog's life** — most shelters do not euthanize pets anymore but some still do.

A word of warning however — while Beagles are loveable additions to families they are not our children! We disrespect them by not allowing them to fully be the creatures they were intended to be. Dogs need a "job to do" in order to be fulfilled, happy companions. **People create "problem dogs"** that fill shelters by asking them to fulfill human emotional needs! Many dogs are asked to be in alpha positions because humans do not understand the nature of the pack. A family is the "pack" to the dog and the dog needs to understand their JOB in the pack. Truly, the only way dogs achieve the respect they deserve is when we allow them to be the creatures they were created to be.

I don't mean to put you off, but consider some factors please before you make this enormous decision. Just think of how awful it would be for a rescued Beagle to be abandoned again because his owners could not cope! This **isn't a way of getting a cheap Beagle** and going in with that mentality is so wrong. Even rescue centers may charge an admin fee, but on top of that there are vaccinations, veterinary bills, worming, spaying or neutering to consider. Can you really afford these?

Sam Goldberg of BeagleHealth.info: "Deciding on whether to adopt an older dog or take a small puppy into your home requires some thought. An older dog doesn't have the teething stage and may well be house trained but can also have some 'baggage' from previous owners. Puppies can be brought up with all the boundaries and rules that you prefer, as well as being fully socialized and having no hang ups. Bringing any Beagle into your home should be clearly discussed beforehand to ensure it is the right breed for you. Of course things can change in any family's life and a new home be needed, and in such a case the new owner should be carefully vetted as you would yourself."

Edy Ballard of Ironwood Beagles: "Rescues are very near and dear to my heart, as I have been involved in Beagle rescue for many years. As with breeders, however, there are good and not-so-good ones. The best rescues have a number of foster homes where the Beagles live until adopted. These foster families evaluate the Beagles for behavioral problems, housetraining, adaptability to children, and many other qualities. However, not all rescue dogs are 'problem dogs.' Some are wonderful dogs whose owners could no longer care for them for a variety of life circumstances, such as relocation, military service, or going into a nursing home. Occasionally rescues get purebred Beagles with papers, pregnant mothers, or puppies. Expect to go through an application process including home evaluation (where many times the rescue will be looking at such things as adequate fencing). Rescue Beagles typically cost $150–300, which includes spay/neuter, microchip, and updating all medical care including vaccines. All in all, the rescue will have far more money invested in each Beagle on average than the adoption fee covers."

One or Two?

When you're confronted with an adorable litter of Beagle puppies, your heart may tell you to go ahead and get two. Listen to your brain! Owning one dog is a serious commitment of time and money, but with two dogs, everything doubles: food, housebreaking, training, vet bills, boarding fees, and time.

While it is true that Beagles are pack animals and love to be a part of a big group, think about your own time and resources. Beagles do fine welcoming a new dog to the family, so I recommend that you start out with just one puppy and see how it goes. You can always add a second Beagle in the future.

Sam Goldberg of BeagleHealth.info: "I very rarely allow someone to buy two Beagles from the same litter. They don't concentrate on the owner at all as they interact with each other, so they need individual time for training and bonding. Adding another once one has an established routine is much easier though, as the second will follow the established daily pattern."

The Need for Socialization

Any breed, no matter how well regarded for its temperament, can still develop bad habits and become obnoxious. Beagle puppies are stubborn, and they do have that inborn hound need to bark and howl. Get on top of that vocal tendency immediately with proper training starting no later than 10–12 weeks of age. (Finish the rabies, distemper, and parvovirus vaccinations before exposing the puppy to other dogs.)

During formal training understand you will be in "school" as much as your Beagle. Dogs will quite happily get away with as much as they can if they get their paws on a compliant human. Your job is to be the "alpha," a responsibility for which many humans are ill-equipped without some in-class time of their own!

Claudia Anderson of TwainHeart Beagles: "Between 8 and 16 weeks is a critical time for puppy socialization. The time and effort you put into this time will pay great rewards during the life of your Beagle. I highly recommend Puppy Kindergarten or some kind of puppy socialization class. These classes give Beagle puppies the opportunity to socialize with other breeds their own age while teaching basic manners. This gives owners a structured approach to working with their puppy and learning techniques to help their puppy become a well-mannered and socialized adult. Contrary to what you may think, dog training is really more about training the people than the dog.

"It's important to find a good trainer to help you. Ask your vet and/or call your local kennel club. Try to find a trainer who is a member of the National Association of Dog Obedience Instructors (NADOI) and/or the Association of Pet Dog Trainers (APDT).

http://www.nadoi.org/
http://www.apdt.com/

"Interview the prospective trainer on the phone and ask about their training techniques. You want a trainer that emphasizes positive rewards for good behavior rather than corrections for bad behavior. Beagles are an odd mix of sensitive and stubborn and do much better when they think the desired behavior is their idea rather than something forced upon them."

Cost of Keeping a Beagle

Being a pet owner is never cheap, especially if you stay up to date with vet appointments and feed your Beagle a high-quality diet. Before you choose to buy or adopt a Beagle, you should make sure that you are able to comfortably cover all of the associated costs.

Upfront costs are the costs you have to cover before you actually bring your Beagle home. This includes things like your Beagle's crate, his food and water dishes, toys, grooming supplies, and the cost of the dog itself. Ongoing expenses include things like veterinary care, vaccinations, dog license, and food.

Photo Credit: Gary Clacher of Misken Beagles.

You will also need to pay for spay/neuter surgery, and microchipping is recommended (and indeed is compulsory in the U.K.). Spay/neuter surgery can be quite expensive if you go to a regular veterinary surgeon, but there are many low-cost clinics that offer spay surgery for $100 to $200 and neuter surgery for as low as $50.

Spay/ neuter in the U.K. will cost upwards of £100 at least and is substantially more in the south than the north.

Having your Beagle microchipped will cost you about $50, but it is well worth it. Each microchip has a unique number that is connected to a profile that includes your contact information. If your Beagle gets lost, whoever finds him can take him to a shelter or vet to get the microchip scanned. Many animal shelters offer microchipping for as little as $15 or microchip them automatically before making them available for adoption.

In addition to the costs already mentioned, you will have to take your Beagle in for regular visits to the vet. When he is a puppy you might have to go every few weeks for vaccinations, but after he turns one year old you'll only need to see the vet every six months or once a year.

Food is the other important recurring cost. Beagles are small dogs, so they do not eat a lot at one time. While you might be able to find a month's supply of dog food for $15, you shouldn't skimp when it comes to your dog's diet. The quality of your Beagle's diet will have a direct impact on his health and wellbeing, so you should choose a high-quality food, even if it costs a little bit more. Giving your dog a healthy diet will cut down on your veterinary costs in the long run because your dog will be healthier.

Pros and Cons of Owning a Beagle

Every breed of dog has its own list of advantages and disadvantages. If you are thinking about buying a Beagle, you would do well to consider both, although it's a very subjective business since what one person may love in a breed another person will not like at all.

People who love Beagles should be ready to talk about their good qualities, as well as the challenges they pose, for one overriding reason — a desire to see these very special animals go to the best home possible where they will be loved and appreciated. I would rather "put someone off" than see a Beagle bought and then slowly neglected over time by a less-than-committed owner.

Pros of Beagle Ownership

- Sturdy, athletic dog in a good, compact size.
- Short coat that needs little maintenance.
- Highly intelligent and loyal.
- Good family dog.
- Active dog that loves the outdoors and exercise.
- Good natured with people but still a good watch dog.
- Easy to housetrain.
- Peaceful with other dogs and sometimes with cats.

Cons of Beagle Ownership

- High exercise needs.
- Stubborn. Obedience training is a must.
- Destructive if bored and can develop separation anxiety.

- Must be kept on a leash and securely fenced, preferably with observation.
- They love to dig and dig!
- Barks, bays, and howls.

Ruth Darlene Stewart of Aladar Beagles: "Beagles are hounds. They live by their nose, stomach and the love of their 'human pack.' Beagle puppies are one of the most adorable puppies to be seen, but are not for everyone. Beagles have a strong sense of smell (as most hound breeds do) and this quality gets them in trouble very often. The first and (in my humble opinion) most important rule for a Beagle owner is to have a SECURE fenced yard. Beagles require lots of activity, and they are not a dog that you can send out on a potty break without an enclosure to contain them. When a Beagle's nose hits the ground there seems to be a disconnect button between the brain and ears. A Beagle must be contained or on leash or its life span will probably be shortened by a car very quickly. Beagles were bred to go find game and the hunter to follow so this trait to follow his nose is just natural.

"Beagles are great pets, but they are also very curious dogs. If a few scratches on the coffee table, dining room table, or frequent emptying of the bathroom trashcan would bother you — THEN A BEAGLE IS NOT FOR YOU. Beagles totally involve themselves in their home and will inspect every inch on a routine basis. If an energetic, intelligent, stubborn, manipulative dog is to be — then the Beagle is the one. Those pleading eyes will melt many hearts.

"Beagles are fun animals to own, but they do have a few bad habits. Stool eating is one of the major drawbacks to owning a Beagle. Not all do this and there are products on the market to help break a Beagle of this habit. I believe it is due to their strong nose and the rich food we feed them.

"Digging also seems to be a part of life with a Beagle. I am constantly amazed how carefully constructive some of my gang's holes are to be exactly in the place where I walk. They dig after grubs and bugs in dirt. A few twisted ankles and I have learned to watch for the holes. Beagles will challenge a fence by digging or climbing to investigate smells. Beagles are 'pack' animals, which means they need and want to be a part of the family. A lonely Beagle left in a backyard will often try to dig out to find humans or other dogs.

"Beagles are also known to be energetic barkers. Some Beagles will bark at the slightest movement or noise, while others seem to care less.

"Beagles are excellent pets for many reasons. They are generally very good with children and require only weekly brushing. Did I mention that Beagles do shed? Beagles are very loving and will charm many a visitor to your house with their antics. Beagles live 10–15 years, and it is very easy to overfeed them due to their constant 'I am starving' attitude. Watching their diet will help to keep them fit and trim. Food is the MAJOR motivator for most Beagles."

Veronica and Rosie Longman of Chatoyant Beagles add: "Beagles are a sensible size, happy, friendly, cheerful hounds. Low maintenance, adaptable, love people especially children. Good 'do-ers,' which makes them easy to own. They do need exercise, training and company, but that to us makes them a good family dog."

Famous Beagles Owners

Beagles are so popular they've even lived in the White House. President Lyndon B. Johnson kept several of the dogs. The ones best known by the public were simply called Him and Her. And let's not forget that the famous character from the Peanuts cartoon, Snoopy, was himself a Beagle. Other "celebrity" Beagle owners include:

- Helio Castroneves
- Barry Manilow
- James Herriott
- Charles Schulz
- Roger Staubach
- Eva Gabor
- Mary Pickford
- Frankie Muniz

Chapter 4 — Buying a Beagle

Now that you have decided to proceed with purchasing a Beagle, for many people who have never purchased a pedigree dog, the process can seem daunting and confusing. How do you select a breeder? How do you know if you're working with a good breeder? How do you pick a puppy? Are you paying a good price?

Pet Quality vs. Show Quality

First, you need to understand the basic terminology you will encounter to rate puppies that are offered for sale by breeders: pet quality and show quality. Understanding the difference in these designations is often as simple as looking at the offered price. Good breeders do what they do for one reason: a desire to improve the breed.

When a puppy is not considered to be a superior example of the breed, the dog will be termed "pet quality." For most of the rest of us, even when the supposed "flaws" are pointed out, all we see is a **wonderfully cute and exuberant puppy**.

You will want a breeder to explain to you why the animal is considered pet quality over show quality, but since reputable breeders don't sell unhealthy dogs, this is not a stumbling block, but rather standard procedure. Pet quality puppies are, by their very definition, judged to be inappropriate for use in breeding programs.

The most obvious reason for wanting to buy a show quality puppy is a desire to get involved in the dog fancy and to exhibit your animal in organized competitions. Show quality animals can cost three times as much or more, so most of us can only afford pet quality pedigree dogs.

Ruth Darlene Stewart of Aladar Beagles: "Pet quality puppies are not inferior puppies — they just have minor imperfections that would keep them from being winners in the show ring. A healthy, well-adjusted, loving Beagle is a winner in anyone's home; regardless of slight imperfections that the average person would not be concerned about or notice. All pet quality puppies (from a reputable breeder) are sold with a spay/neuter contract and on a limited registration. Written contracts should be required on all show and pet puppies sold. Health guarantees should be included in the contracts, as well as stipulations that the Beagle may not be resold, given away, taken to a shelter, etc. If for any reason a buyer of one of my puppies cannot keep it, the puppy comes back to me or I have approval of to whom it goes. I take lifetime responsibility for each puppy I produce — regardless of age.

"Color, sex, and size are all personal preferences. I encourage prospective Beagles owners to also consider obtaining an older dog or a rescue dog. There are many advantages to obtaining an older dog or rescue Beagle. Many dogs that have obtained their championship or that have not grown up to the potential seen as a puppy are available from breeders. These dogs are already crate trained, leashed broken, socialized, the teething stage is over (your furniture will love that), and usually they are also housebroken. Please consider bringing an older Beagle into your home or better yet providing a home for one of the rescue Beagles available."

How Much Do They Cost?

Prices vary widely. Beagle puppies for sale from reputable breeders cost approximately $750-$2000. In the U.K., a carefully bred Kennel

Club registered Beagle will cost in the region of £800 to £950. Most breeders do not list prices on their home pages.

Heather and Robert Lindberg of Windstar Beagles say: "For a well-bred Beagle pet you should expect to spend around $1500. The expense of health testing and the time invested in a properly bred and socialized puppy is well worth the cost."

We have worked together with many of the best Beagle breeders in producing this book. We asked them about their pricing and the consensus was that when looking at the price of a Beagle, one must keep in mind all the costs incurred by a reputable breeder versus a puppy mill. No matter what the initial price, remember this is **nothing compared** to the long-term ongoing costs of dog ownership.

Sadly, unscrupulous breeders with almost no knowledge of the breed

Photo Credit: Andrew and Tanya Gittins of Boomerloo Beagles.

have sprung up, tempted by the prospect of making easy money. A healthy Beagle will be an irreplaceable part of your family for the next decade or more. You shouldn't buy an unseen or imported puppy, or one from a pet shop or newspaper! You may end up saving a small amount in the short term only to find you have a puppy that has potential health issues that will cost you **thousands** more in the long run.

A **suspiciously low** price means that Beagle is most likely from a "puppy mill" (think factory) where corners are cut, annual specialist exams do not happen, breeders continue to use parent dogs with genetic problems, and puppies are usually crated for the first 8 weeks and kept in isolation, meaning no socialization, which could lead to behavioral problems that you get stuck with.

What is important is to ask the breeders about the **testing they do on the parent dogs**, and to ask what the guarantee is against health problems. Get this **in writing before you buy**. You need to base your decision on QUALITY and not price!

Good Beagle breeders usually have a waiting list of prospective owners and **do not sell their dogs to anyone**. Of course it may be possible to browse the internet or the local classified adverts and see lower prices, but quality breeding comes at a cost, and if a Beagle puppy is being sold for less, question why.

The Kennel Club has conducted research with shocking results. Too many people are still going to unscrupulous breeders, with:

• One third of people failing to see the puppy with its mother
• More than half not seeing the breeding environment
• 70% receive no contract of sale
• 82% not offered post-sales advice
• 69% not seeing any relevant health certificates for the puppy's parents, which indicate the likely health of the puppy

Obviously we have made clear that finding reputable breeders is your best way to find a puppy, but these websites may also help:

American Kennel Club marketplace — http://marketplace.akc.org/
Adopt a Pet — http://www.adoptapet.com
Petango — http://www.petango.com
Puppy Find — http://www.puppyfind.com/
Oodle — http://dogs.oodle.com/
The U.K. Kennel Club —
https://www.thekennelclub.org.uk/services/public/findapuppy/
NBC member breeders alphabetized by state —
https://www.nationalbeagleclub.org/Breeders

In the U.K., **The Kennel Club Assured Breeder Scheme** promotes good breeding practice and aims to work together with breeders and buyers to force irresponsible breeders, or puppy farmers, out of business. Every single Assured Breeder is inspected by the Kennel Club, a U.K.

AS-accredited certification body, in order to ensure that the Scheme is upheld as the essential quality seal for puppy breeding and buying.

Ruth Darlene Stewart of Aladar Beagles: "The purchase price of a puppy is just about the last question you should ask a breeder. Yes, we all like to save money, but the time to do it is not when you buy your puppy. You'll almost certainly regret it later.

"A responsible breeder put the best genetic material into building your puppy when she chose the sire and dam. She didn't just breed your pup's mother to the dog down the block because he was handy. She studied pedigrees and temperaments and faults and virtues and chose the particular sire that would produce the best puppies when bred to that particular bitch.

"Both parents were likely tested for genetic defects specific to Beagles. These problems are not always evident at birth, but can crop up several years later in the most heartbreaking ways. A good breeder cannot absolutely guarantee against all genetic defects, but has chosen as carefully as possible to minimize the possibility of your puppy having them. Before you buy a puppy, you should study the breed carefully and find out what the breed's problems are and whether pre-breeding screening is available.

"The mother receives the absolute best prenatal care available, with no expense spared. When the puppies arrive, they are treated the same way. They not only are physically healthy, but are properly socialized and checked for sound temperaments. They receive recommended vaccinations and are checked and treated for worms and other parasites. Show prospects and pets from the litter receive exactly the same care.

"When you take your puppy home, it's with a health guarantee and your most valuable resource — instructions to call the breeder with any questions. Having problems housebreaking? Call the breeder. Wonder if a behavior is normal? Call the breeder. Puppy is off his feed? Call the breeder. There is no question so trivial that a good breeder is not interested in helping you find the answer.

"Seldom does a good breeder make a profit on a litter of puppies. What may seem like a large purchase price to you is only a drop in the bucket of expenses the breeder faces in planning a litter. You aren't lining the breeder's pockets when you buy a quality puppy. You are simply helping her continue to afford to breed. Reputable breeders do not breed for the money, but not many of them could afford to breed if they didn't cover at least part of the expenses through pet sales."

How to Choose a Breeder

Typically, the first step in finding a specific type of puppy is tracking down a breeder. Thankfully, this is hardly a problem with a breed as popular as the Beagle.

Visit breeder websites and speak over the phone to breeders in whose dogs you are interested before you schedule a puppy visit. You want a breeder who is clearly serious about their breeding program and displays this fact with copious information about their dogs, including lots and lots of pictures.

Photo Credit: Stacey Burrows of Summerlily Beagles.

You should evaluate the breeder's knowledge not only of the breeding process but of the Beagle breed specifically. Avoid any that seem **unwilling** to answer your questions and those who do not seem to have the best interest of their puppies in mind. Plan on visiting more than one before you make your decision. **Never** buy a Beagle that is less than 8 weeks old or one that has not been fully weaned.

Finding advertisements for Beagles in local newspapers or similar publications is **dicey at best**. All too often, if you go through the classified ads you can stumble upon a puppy mill where dogs are being raised in deplorable conditions for profit only.

Never buy any dog unless you can meet the parents and siblings and see for yourself the surroundings in which the dog was born and is being raised. If you are faced with having to travel to pick up your dog, it's a huge advantage to see recorded video footage, or to do a live videoconference with the breeder and the puppies.

It is far preferable to work with a breeder from whom you can verify the health of the parents and discuss the potential for any congenital illnesses. Responsible breeders are **more than willing** to give you all this information and more, and are actively interested in making sure their dogs go to good homes. If you don't get this "vibe" from someone seeking to sell you a dog, something is wrong.

I'm not a great fan of shipping live animals. If possible, try finding a local breeder, or one in reasonable traveling distance. Even if you find a Beagle breeder online, visit the breeder at least once before you buy. Plan on picking your Beagle up in person from the breeder.

Note that the Animal Care Welfare Act passed in November 2013 gives new laws/guidelines for breeders who ship. They now need to be **federally licensed** by the USDA.

Be suspicious of any breeder unwilling to allow such a visit or one who doesn't want to show you around their operation. You don't want to interact with just one puppy. You **should meet the parent(s)** and the entire litter.

It's important to get a sense of how the dogs live, and their level of care. When you talk to the breeder, information should flow in both directions. The breeder should discuss both the positives and negatives associated with the dogs.

Nowadays many breeders are home-based, and their dogs live in the house as pets. Puppies are typically raised in the breeder's home as well. It's also very common for Beagle breeders to use **guardian homes** for their breeding dogs. The breeder retains ownership of the dog during the years the dog is used for breeding, but the dog lives permanently with the guardian family. This arrangement is great for the dog because once retired from breeding he/she is spayed/neutered and returned to its forever family. There is no need to re-home the dog after its breeding career has ended.

Edy Ballard of Ironwood Beagles: "You usually won't be able to see both parents, just the dam (mother). Often the bitch is sent away to an outside stud dog to be bred. Rarely does a breeder breed his own bitch to his own dog. However, you should be able to see photos of the sire and a 5-generation pedigree.

"It's very important to understand that **you probably won't be able to pick out your puppy** if purchasing from a show breeder. Show breeders breed to have something to show. To that end, they will usually select and keep the most promising show prospect. Other show prospects may be reserved for other show homes. Of the remaining puppies, the experienced breeder will select the best puppy for your home and family based on your needs. For example, the boldest, most playful puppy may be best for a family with active children, whereas a shy or quiet puppy would be better suited to a retired couple."

What to Expect from a Good Breeder

Responsible breeders help you select a puppy. They place the long-term welfare of the dog front and center. The owner should show interest in your life and ask questions about your schedule, family, and other pets. This is not nosiness. It is an excellent sign that you are working with a professional with a genuine interest in placing their dogs appropriately. Owners who aren't interested in what kind of home the Beagle will have are suspect.

When you go to look at puppies, take your lifestyle into consideration. Pick the puppy that will fit in your household. For example, if you have a quiet household and want a lap dog, or just want to take walks with the dog, pick the puppy with the laid-back personality. They will be content to sit with you more. If you have active children and want a dog to play fetch with them, pick the busy puppy.

You want the breeder to be a resource for you in the future if you need help or guidance in living with your Beagle. Be receptive to answering your breeder's queries and open to having an ongoing friendship. It is quite common for breeders to call and check on how their dogs are doing and to make themselves available to answer questions.

I strongly recommend that you take your newly-purchased puppy to a vet to have a **thorough check-up within 48 hours**. If there are any issues with the health of the puppy, it will be difficult emotionally but worth it to return him to save you from a lifetime of pain, as well as the financial costs in vet bills. Good breeders will have a guarantee for this eventuality in their contract.

Good Breeders Checklist

1. Check that the area where the puppies are kept is clean and that the puppies themselves look clean.

2. They don't breed multiple breeds: 2 or 3 maximum. Ideally they only breed and specialize in the Beagle.

3. Their Beagles are alert and appear happy and excited to meet you.

4. Puppies are not always available on tap but instead they have a waiting list of interested purchasers.

5. They don't over-breed, because this can be detrimental to the female's health.

6. They ask you lots of questions about you and your home.

7. They feed their Beagles a high quality "premium" dog food or possibly even a raw diet.

8. They freely offer great specific, detailed advice and indicate that they are on hand after the sale to help with any questions.

9. You get to meet the mother when you visit.

10. You are not rushed in and out, but get to spend time with the dogs and are able to revisit for a second time if necessary.

11. They provide a written contract and health guarantees.

12. They have health records for your puppy showing visits to the vet, vaccinations, worming, etc. and certificates to show he is free from genetic defects.

13. They clearly explain what you need to do once you get your puppy home.

14. They agree to take the puppy back if necessary.

15. They are part of official organizations or have accreditations.

16. They have been breeding Beagles for a number of years.

17. They allow you to speak to previous customers.

18. When selling a purebred (pedigree) Beagle, the breeder is willing to provide original official AKC or Kennel Club papers to prove registration.

The Breeder Should Provide the Following

In the best cases, transactions with good breeders include the following components:

- The *contract of sale* details both parties' responsibilities. It also explains the transfer of paperwork and records.

- The *information packet* offers feeding, training, and exercise advice. It also recommends standard procedures like worming and vaccinations.

- The *description of ancestry* includes the names and types of Beagle used in breeding.

- *Health records* detail medical procedures, include vaccination records, and disclose potential genetic issues.

- The breeder should *guarantee the puppy's health* at the time of pick up. You will be required to confirm this fact with a vet within a set period of time.

Photo Credit: Diana Brown of Raimex Beagles.

8 Warning Signs of a Potential Bad Breeder

Always be alert to key warning signs like:

1. Breeders who tell you it is not necessary for you to visit their facility in person.

2. Assertions that you can buy a puppy sight unseen with confidence.

3. Breeders who will allow you to come to their home or facility, but who will not show you where the Beagles actually live.

4. Dogs kept in dirty, overcrowded conditions where the animals seem nervous and apprehensive.

5. Situations in which you are not allowed to meet at least one of the puppies' parents.

6. Sellers who can't produce health information or that say they will provide the records later.

7. No health guarantee and no discussion of what happens if the puppy does fall ill, including a potential refund.

8. Refusal to provide a signed bill of sale or vague promises to forward one later.

Puppy Mills

Such operations **exist for profit only**. They crank out the greatest number of litters possible with an eye toward nothing but the bottom line. The care the dogs receive ranges from deplorable to **non-existent**. Inbreeding is standard, leading to genetic abnormalities, wide-ranging health problems, and short lifespan.

The internet is, unfortunately, a ripe advertising ground for puppy mills, as are pet shops. If you can't afford to buy from a reputable breeder, consider a shelter or rescue dog: you are saving an animal in need.

Be **highly suspicious** of any breeder that assures you they have dogs available at all times. It is normal, and a sign that you are working with a reputable breeder, for your name to be placed on a waiting list. You may also be asked to place a small deposit to guarantee that you can buy a puppy from a coming litter. Should you choose not to take one of the dogs, this money is generally refunded, but find out the terms of such a transaction in advance.

Again, something is wrong if you can't:

- visit the facility where the puppies were born
- meet the parents
- inspect the facilities
- receive some genetic and health information

Avoiding Scams

It's so easy to get emotionally charged up about getting a beautiful puppy, and getting really hooked by photos on a website. But, sadly, many people have done just that, and ended up with a puppy that had to be put down because of a serious heart defect, or have extremely expensive surgery to correct patellar luxation, and the seller has offered no refund, full or partial. Parent dogs that are being mated should have been screened for genetic faults prior to being bred.

Many people have paid a lot for a puppy only to discover it has temperament disorders that cannot be corrected, after spending many thousands of dollars with professional trainers. This is all so avoidable.

People need to know about the health guarantee the breeder offers. What does it cover? All genetic faults? Do you have to return the puppy to the breeder as part of the health guarantee? This is how many breeders get out of honoring their guarantee. They know the buyer will be way too attached to the puppy to return it in order to get the refund. The refund should go toward the cost of surgery to repair the patella or whatever health fault needs medical attention.

Always buy from a breeder that has verifiable references from professional trainers or vets. Do a search on the Better Business Bureau website to confirm that the business has no complaints or has settled all complaints.

Verify the breeder's reputation by speaking with other families that have adopted puppies from them to make sure the puppies come from quality adult breeding dogs and that the breeder is honest and ethical. Ask to see the buyer's contract and health warranty documents BEFORE you buy. Go by contract and not just conversation.

Deal directly with your breeder and avoid any middlemen. When considering any business, BE SURE to do a Google search for the business or the website name followed by the words "complaints" or "reviews." If there have been problems, various websites for rip-off reporting and consumer complaints will come up.

Edy Ballard of Ironwood Beagles: "Choose a breeder you feel comfortable and can develop a relationship with. This person should be a resource to you for the life of your new Beagle. Many of my puppy buyers have become lifelong friends. A good breeder will want to know how your dog is doing as it grows and matures."

Identification Systems for Dogs

Your Beagle may or may not have a means of permanent identification on their bodies when they are purchased. Governing organizations use

differing systems. The American Kennel Club recommends permanent identification as a "common sense" practice. The preferred options are tattoos or microchips.

Microchipping is perfectly safe and involves implanting a small transponder inside a glass capsule around the size of a grain of rice under the skin between the shoulder blades. When a scanner is passed over the chip a unique number comes up to identify the registered owner (make sure to remember to keep your contact details updated).

Photo Credit: Peter and Val Davies of Barrvale Beagles.

Since 2016, microchipping has been made compulsory in the U.K. for all dogs. All puppies sold **have to be** microchipped by 8 weeks of age, i.e., prior to purchase by new owners. You must have this done by an authorized implanter. Failure to do so will result in a £500 fine if caught and prosecuted.

Costs are not expensive — from trained and licensed microchippers who charge around £15 to vets costing around £25.

Any dogs traveling to or returning to the U.K. from another country can do so under the Pet Passport system, for which microchipping is a requirement. For more information, see http://www.gov.uk/take-pet-abroad.

What Is the Best Age to Purchase a Puppy?

Beagle puppies are born with their eyes and ears closed. Newborn puppies have no teeth and very little fur, so they rely completely on their mother for warmth.

Sandra Groeschel of The Whim says: "Here in the U.S., the Beagle litters number 4–6 puppies averaging 8–10 oz each. Litters do not favor males vs females."

Joan Wurst of Everwind Beagles: "My puppies generally weigh approximately between ¾ of a pound and a pound at birth. Of course there will be those that may weigh a bit more. I start my puppies on their vaccines at six weeks."

Gary Clacher of Misken Beagles: "On size of newborns … my smallest has been 200 grams, largest 425 grams."

A Beagle puppy needs time to learn important life skills from the mother dog, including eating solid food and grooming themselves. For this reason, it is harmful to bring puppies to your home too early. These are the key puppy stages.

0–7 Weeks

Puppies typically open their eyes at 14 days, and the ears will also open two weeks after birth. Puppies rely on their mothers not only for warmth during the first few weeks but also for food — they will spend about 90% of their day sleeping and 10% feeding.

Puppies live on a mother's milk-only diet for approximately the first 4 weeks. He learns discipline and manners from his mother, and littermates help with socialization and learning the social rules of the pack.

A mother will start to self-wean her pups when they are about four weeks old. You can tell when she is ready because she will not want to spend much time in the box with them. As the puppies' teeth emerge, the dam will be more reluctant to nurse. This is normal and helps her milk production start to slow down. At this point it is important for the breeder to start supplementing the puppies with a good quality puppy food mixture four times per day. Usually by seven or eight weeks, the puppies are fully weaned from the mother's milk.

Puppies are not able to control their bowels when they are first born, so the mother will lick them to help stimulate urination and defecation.

8–12 Weeks

At about eight weeks the puppies will receive their first vaccine. Because it is not known exactly when the maternal antibodies from the mother's milk will wear off, a series of vaccines is required. Your veterinarian will give you the best recommendations.

The fact is that most puppies go home at eight weeks, but none should ever go sooner than this, as this could result in negative issues such as shyness. A "breeder" doing this may simply want to cash in and turn over lots of puppies too quickly.

From the time the puppies are weaned at about eight weeks, until they are ready for their new homes, their mother and siblings continue to teach them "dog manners." A good breeder will also start basic leash and crate training during the first 8–12 weeks. This helps the puppy adjust to its new home much easier!

Now that the brain is developed, he needs socializing with the outside world, otherwise he can become fearful.

12 Weeks Onwards

Some breeders will insist on keeping the puppies longer (10–12 weeks) to allow the puppy's immune system to become stronger.

During your puppy's change to adolescence, continue exposure to as many different sounds, smells, and people as possible. Begin formal training and obedience, and always praise his good behavior without being too strict or too soft with him.

How to Choose a Puppy?

My best advice is to go with the puppy that is drawn to you. My standard strategy in selecting a pup has always been to sit a little apart from a litter and let one of the dogs come to me. My late father was, in his own way, a "dog whisperer." He taught me this trick for picking puppies, and it's never let me down.

Photo Credit: Edy Ballard of Ironwood Beagles.

I've had dogs in my life since childhood and enjoyed a special connection with them all. I will say that often the dog that comes to me isn't the one I might have chosen — but I still consistently rely on this method.

You will want to choose a puppy with a friendly, easy-going temperament, and your breeder should be able to help you with your selection. Also ask the breeder about the temperament and personalities of the puppy's parents and if they have socialized the puppies.

Always be certain to ask if a Beagle puppy you are interested in has displayed any signs of aggression or fear, because if this is happening at such an early age, you may experience behavioral troubles as the puppy becomes older.

Beyond this, I suggest that you interact with your dog with a clear understanding that **each one is an individual** with unique traits. It is not so much a matter of learning about all Beagles, but rather of learning about YOUR Beagle dog.

9 Essential Health Tests You Can Use

Before the "Aw Factor" kicks in and you are completely swept away by the cuteness of a Beagle puppy, familiarize yourself with some basic quick health checks.

1. Although a puppy may be sleepy at first, the dog should wake up quickly and be both alert and energetic.

2. The little dog should feel well fed in your hands, with some fat over the rib area.

3. The coat should be shiny and healthy with no dandruff, bald patches, or greasiness.

4. The puppy should walk and run easily and energetically with no physical difficulty or impairment.

5. The eyes should be bright and clear with no sign of discharge or crustiness.

6. Breathing should be quiet, with no sneezing or coughing and no discharge or crust on the nostrils.

7. Examine the area around the genitals to ensure there is no visible fecal collection or accumulation of pus. If a puppy is dirty from pee or fecal matter then that, for me, is reason to leave quickly without wasting any more of your time, as it indicates poor standards.

8. Test the dog's hearing by clapping your hands when the puppy is looking away from you and judge the puppy's reaction.

9. Test the vision by rolling a ball toward the dog, making sure the puppy appropriately notices and interacts with the object.

6 Great Checks for Puppy Social Skills

When choosing a Beagle puppy out of a litter, look for one that is friendly and outgoing, rather than one who is overly aggressive or fearful. Puppies who demonstrate good social skills with their littermates are much more likely to develop into easy-going, happy adult dogs that play well with others.

Observe all the puppies together and take notice:

1. Which puppies are comfortable both on top and on the bottom when play fighting and wrestling with their littermates? Which puppies seem to only like being on top?

2. Which puppies try to keep the toys away from the other puppies, and which puppies share?

3. Which puppies seem to like the company of their littermates, and which ones seem to be loners?

4. Puppies that ease up or stop rough play when another puppy yelps or cries are more likely to respond appropriately when they play too roughly as adults.

5. Is the puppy sociable with humans? If they will not come to you, or display fear toward strangers, this could develop into a problem later in their life.

6. Is the puppy relaxed about being handled? If not, they may become difficult with adults and children during daily interactions, grooming, or visits to the veterinarian's office.

Submissive or Dominant?

It is something of a myth that dogs are either submissive or dominant. In reality, they are likely to be somewhere in between the two, but it is helpful to understand where they fit in so you know how to deal with them. Watching how they act around their littermates can give you clues.

Submissive dogs:

• Turn away when other dogs stare
• Are happy to play with their littermates
• Do not try to dominate other dogs
• May show submissive urination when greeting other dogs
• Allow other dogs to win at tug-of-war
• Provide attention and affection to other dogs
• Back off when other dogs want to take food or toys
• Roll on their backs to display their belly

If a Beagle shows definite submissive or dominant tendencies, which should you pick? There is no one right answer. You need to choose a puppy that best suits your family's lifestyle.

A submissive Beagle will naturally be more passive, less manic, and possibly easier to train. A dominant Beagle will usually be more energetic and lively. They could be more stubborn and difficult to train or socialize, but this needn't be a negative and can be overcome with a little persistence.

Dogs are pack animals, and they are happiest when they have structure and they can follow their nature. Followers want to be told what to do and know what the leaders expect of them. Know that you must be the pack leader to your Beagle. He should be submissive even to younger children, so aggression and other problem behaviors don't arise.

Chapter 5 — Caring for Your New Beagle Puppy

All puppies are forces of nature, and Beagles are no exception. The first four months of any dog's life is a critical period for training and socialization. In a dog like the Beagle that is both social and extremely active, you have a breed that needs to be a companion and needs a "job."

Photo Credit: Rachel Southammavong of South Beagles.

A bored Beagle is a destructive Beagle. During these early months your new pet must learn to be crated while you are away to prevent destructive behavior, separation anxiety, barking, and howling. A tiny puppy throwing his head back and baying may be cute, but the vocalization is disastrous in a grown dog. Never encourage your Beagle to howl by howling with him!

A Beagle's native curiosity and his determination to check out new smells paired with his obstinate nature make puppy proofing your home all the more important. Normal chewing, on appropriate toys, is a healthy activity for any dog. Your job is to put a stop to destructive chewing before it becomes a life habit.

Beagles can easily become proficient beggars and without proper exercise, they pack on the pounds quickly. Put your foot down from the start and do not allow your dog to develop a fondness for human foods, and keep up your end of the bargain by making sure your dog gets the activity he needs.

Beagles can live as long as 15 years. Don't let any bad habits get started when your dog is a puppy, or you could be dealing with the consequences for a long time!

Household Poisons

A dog, especially a young one, will eat pretty much anything, often gulping something down with no forethought. Take a complete inventory of the areas to which the dog will have access. Remove all lurking poisonous dangers from cabinets and shelves. Get everything up and out of the dog's reach. Pay special attention to:

- cleaning products
- insecticides
- mothballs
- fertilizers
- antifreeze

If you are not sure about any item, assume it's poisonous and remove it.

Look Through Your Beagle's Eyes

Think of a puppy as a bright toddler with four legs. Get yourself in the mindset that you're bringing a baby genius home, and try to think like a puppy. Every nook and cranny invites exploration. Every discovery can then be potentially chewed, swallowed — or both!

Get down on the floor and have a look around from puppy level. Your new furry Einstein will spot anything that catches your attention and many things that don't!

Do not leave any dangling electrical cords, drapery pulls, or even loose scraps of wallpaper. Look for forgotten items that have gotten wedged behind cushions or kicked under the furniture. Don't let anything stay out that could be a choking hazard.

Tie up anything that might create a **"topple" danger**. A coaxial cable may look boring to you, but in the mouth of a determined little dog, it could send a heavy television set crashing down. Cord minders and electrical ties are your friends!

Remove stuffed items and pillows, and cover the legs of prized pieces of furniture against chewing. Take anything out of the room that even looks like it **might** be a toy. Think I'm kidding? Go online and do a Google image search for "dog chewed cell phone" and shudder at what you will see.

Bowel blockages can occur from a Beagle eating foreign objects they cannot pass. Some Beagles are chewers. You must be careful about leaving things on the floor or within reach of them. Rope toys, some hard plastic or rubber bones, towels, or any material with string can be deadly to a dog.

If you suspect your pup or dog has eaten something, call your vet immediately, as this could require surgery. Your vet may instruct you to induce vomiting to get it up first. If you see that your dog has no interest in eating, or eats and vomits, it could have a blockage. They may be lethargic. They may also have a tender belly if you rub it. All these are reason for concern.

I stopped using towels as bedding many years ago, as one dog ate part of a towel and could not pass it. The string acts like a saw in the intestines. This can be deadly. I recommend replacing bedding with fleece blankets. They have no string, and if a dog chews it up it will pass the material.

Plant Dangers, Inside and Out

The list of indoor and outdoor plants that are a toxic risk to dogs is long and includes many surprises. You may know that apricot and peach pits are poisonous to canines, but what about spinach and tomato vines? The **American Society for the Prevention of Cruelty to Animals** has created a large reference list of plants for dog owners here:

https://www.aspca.org/pet-care/animal-poison-control/toxic-and-non-toxic-plants

Go through the list and remove any plants from your home that might make your puppy sick. Don't just assume that your dog will leave such items alone.

Sam Goldberg of BeagleHealth.info: "If your puppy (or adult Beagle) eats anything that you are unsure of it is best to ring for advice. Some unexpected things can be toxic to dogs such as grapes and onions and may make your dog very ill if they consume them."

What to Name Your Beagle?

Have you thought of a name yet? Here are our best breeder tips:

1. Choose something you're not embarrassed to shout out loud in public.
2. The shorter the better. Dogs find names with 1 or 2 syllables easiest to recognize, e.g., Lucky.
3. Long names inevitably end up being shortened so think what they could be now — do you like them?
4. Names starting with s, sh, ch, k, etc. are good because dogs hear high frequency sounds best.
5. Ending with a vowel works well, particularly a short "a" or a long "e" sound.
6. Avoid popular and cliché names.
7. Don't go for a name that sounds similar to a command.
8. If you take ownership of a Beagle that already has a name, keep the new one similar sounding for his sake.

Preparing for the Homecoming

Don't give a young Beagle full run of the house before it is housetrained. Keep your new pet confined to a designated area behind a baby gate. This protects your home and possessions and keeps the dog safe from hazards like staircases. Depending on the size and configuration, baby gates retail from $25-$100 / £15-£60.

Before you bring your new puppy home, buy an appropriate travel crate and a wire crate for home use. Since the home crate will also be an important tool in housebreaking, the size of the unit is important.

Many pet owners want to get a crate large enough for the puppy to "grow into" in the interest of saving money. When you are housebreaking a dog, you are working with the principle that the animal will not soil its own "den." If you buy a huge crate for a small dog, the puppy is likely to pick a corner as the "bathroom," thus setting back his training.

Crates are rated by the size of the dog in pounds / kilograms. The commonly suggested crate sizes by weight are:

- 19" x 12" x 15" / 48.26 cm x 30.48 cm x 38.1 cm-10 lbs. /4.53 kg
- 24" x 18" x 20" / 60.96 cm x 45.72 cm x 50.8 cm-25 lbs. / 11.34 kg
- 30" x 19" x 22" / 76.20 cm x 48.26 cm x 55.9 cm-40 lbs. / 18.14 kg
- 35.5" x 22" x 24" / 90.17 cm x 55.88 cm x 60.96 cm-70 lbs. / 31.75 kg
- 42" x 28" x 31" / 106.68 cm x 71.12 cm x 78.74 cm-90 lbs. / 40.83 kg
- 48" x 30" x 33" / 121.92 cm x 76.20 cm x 83.82 cm-110 lbs. / 49.90 kg

Put one or two puppy-safe chew toys in the crate for the ride home along with a recently worn article of clothing. You want the dog to learn your scent. Be sure to fasten the seat belt over the crate.

Sam Goldberg of BeagleHealth.info: "In the U.K. Croft are a good source of crates — they have a range of sizes and types to suit all pockets: www.croftonline.co.uk.

"Crates are really good things. They are not a prison at all but a safe den for your new Beagle to go to when they are tired and would like to rest. They are also good for travelling and visiting friends who may not want your new Beagle cruising around the house. I find friends are not so bothered about Beagle visits if they are quietly sitting in a crate."

Edy Ballard of Ironwood Beagles: "A good breeder will begin crate training and get your puppy accustomed to sleeping alone in his crate. Ironwood puppies get lots of car rides (again, in a crate for safety) and become introduced to a soft collar and leash. All Ironwood puppies go home with a blanket and a small amount of the food they are fed while here."

Talk to the breeder to ensure your Beagle doesn't eat too close to the journey so there is less chance of car sickness, and when he arrives at your home he will be hungry — always a good start!

It is also a nice touch to get an **old rag or towel** from your breeder that has been with the dam. Leave this with your puppy for the first few days, as her scent will help him to settle in more easily.

Take your puppy out to do its business before putting it in the crate. Expect whining and crying. **Don't give in!** Leave them in the crate! It's far safer for the puppy to ride there than to be on someone's lap. Try if possible to take someone with you to sit next to the crate and comfort the puppy while you drive.

Don't overload the dog's senses with too many people. No matter how excited the kids may be at the prospect of a new puppy, leave the children back at the house. The trip home needs to be calm and quiet.

You may need to make a stop, depending on the length of journey. He will likely be nervous, so cover the bottom of the crate with newspapers or a towel just in case. **Have water** and give him a drink en route.

As soon as you arrive home, take your Beagle puppy to a patch of grass outside so he can relieve himself. Immediately **begin encouraging** him for doing so. Dogs are pack animals with an innate desire to please their "leader." Positive and consistent praise is an important part of housebreaking.

Although a gregarious breed, Beagles can easily be overwhelmed and nervous in new surroundings. This is especially true of a puppy away from its mother and littermates for the first time. Stick with the usual feeding schedule, and use the same kind of food the dog has been receiving at the breeder's, because their digestive systems cannot cope with a sudden change.

Create a designated "puppy-safe" area in the house and let the puppy explore on its own. Don't isolate the little dog, but don't overwhelm it either. Resist the urge to pick up the puppy every time it cries.

Give the dog soft pieces of worn clothing to further familiarize him with your scent. Leave a radio playing at a low volume for "company."

At night you may opt to give the baby a well-wrapped warm water bottle, but put the dog in its crate and do not bring it to bed with you. I realize that last bit may sound all but impossible, but if you want a crate-trained dog, you have to **start from day one**. It's much, much harder to get a dog used to sleeping overnight in his crate after any time in the bed with you.

I also suggest you **take some time off work**. For about two weeks this will be your full-time job! Constant supervision is essential to housetrain your puppy quickly and to give him company while he gets accustomed to his new home, which can be overwhelming initially.

Remember that your new puppy is essentially a newborn baby — they need a lot of sleep! Puppies need their nap time, especially after playing. Also, in the evening keep them up with you so when you are ready to go to bed the pup is as well.

It is also likely they will whine for the first few days as they adapt to their new surroundings. They may well follow you around the house constantly. Just handle them gently, make them comfortable, and give them peace and quiet and allow them to sleep as much as they need.

They may also shiver and not eat. Of course, this is all very stressful for you, but don't panic. Obviously ensure they are not in a cold place, and put warm blankets in their crate or bed. Your Beagle will eat eventually.

Try taking the food away if they are not ready to eat, then the next time you put something down for him, he is more likely to be hungry.

Photo Credit: Teresa Gaier of Copper Rose Beagles.

The Importance of the Crate

The crate plays an important role in your dog's life. Historically crates have been more popular in America than in Europe, however, this attitude is slowly changing. Don't think of its use as "imprisoning" your Beagle. The dog sees the crate as a den and will retreat to it for safety and security. Beagles often go to their crates just to enjoy quiet time like we humans do from time to time!

When you accustom your dog to a crate as a puppy, you **get ahead** of issues of separation anxiety and prepare your pet to do well with travel. The crate also plays an important role in housebreaking.

Never rush crate training. Don't lose your temper or show frustration. The Beagle must go into the crate on its own. Begin by leaving the door open. Tie it in place so it does not slam shut by accident. Give your puppy a treat each time he goes inside. Reinforce his good behavior with verbal praise.

Never use the crate as punishment. Proper use of the crate gives both you and your Beagle peace of mind. In time with some patience and training, he will regard the crate **as his special place** in the house.

Some breeders **recommend two crates**, one within earshot or inside the bedroom of a family member, and then the other crate in a medium traffic area on the main floor. You want one that comes with a divider; I block off 2/3 of the crate and only use 1/3. If you don't do this, the puppy goes to the corner and pees and poops there, totally stopping progress for potty training.

I can also recommend a product called Snuggle Puppy. They are great for calming the puppy in the crate — couple that with a covered crate and the puppy goes right to sleep. Exercise, covered crate and Snuggle Puppy = sound asleep puppy in under two minutes!

From SmartPetLove.com: "Our products incorporate the real-feel pulsing heartbeat technology and warmth to help soothe your pet."

Sam Goldberg of BeagleHealth.info: "A little time alone is also good, as Beagles can quickly become used to having constant company. There will always be a family emergency when the Beagle can't come and being able to settle quietly on their own for an hour or so is essential."

Edy Ballard of Ironwood Beagles: "Never, never, never use the crate as a form of punishment. The crate should always be associated with rest and pleasant experiences. It's your puppy's den and a place where she can go to get some quiet time. Never toss puppy into her crate out of frustration or anger."

Our Top 10 Crate Training Tips:

1. Beagles like to be near their family, so initially he will whine and cry simply because he is separated from you and not because he is in "a cage." Remember that any sort of

interaction, positive or negative, will be a "reward" to him, so ignore the whining.

2. Give your Beagle enough room to turn around in. They appreciate space.

3. Always ensure there is access to fresh water inside the crate.

4. Don't keep them locked up in their crate all day just because you have to go to work — this is unfair.

5. Young puppies shouldn't spend more than 2–3 hours in the crate without a toilet break, as they cannot last that long without relieving themselves. This means you should take them out for toilet breaks during the night.

6. Don't place the crate in a draughty place or in direct sunlight where he could overheat. A constant temperature is best. A metal wire crate (compared to plastic) is best so air flows through the gaps.

7. Making the crate his bed from day one is best. Put in some bedding so he feels comfortable and warm at night.

8. Initially to crate train him, put some tasty treats in the crate and leave the door open when he dashes in excitedly! Also be sure to feed him his meals in the crate so he associates it with positive emotions. Don't shut the door yet, as that will introduce a negative aspect. Let him roam in and out, being rewarded with treats when he goes into the crate.

9. After a few days, you can begin closing the door for short periods while he is eating. Get ready for some possible whining but remember to stay strong! Some treats pushed through the wire as a reward works well.

10. To begin with, just close the door for a minute, no more. In a few days, increase the time gradually so he slowly gets accustomed to the door being closed.

Where Should They Sleep?

I have established that I am firmly behind the use of a crate, but you can also have a bed if you prefer, but most importantly — where will your Beagle sleep?

I know some new owners can't resist having them in their beds, but I strongly suggest not giving into this! Yes, they will whine and cry for the first couple of nights, but **this will stop!** Sleeping in your bed could be dangerous: they might wet the bed, and with their relatively short legs **it is potentially dangerous** for them to jump on and off the bed.

I don't recommend it but yes, you could have the crate in the bedroom initially, but why not just start as you mean to go on from day one? Place the crate downstairs I say, and your life will be so much easier once they settle in after a few days.

Go Slow with the Children

If you have children, talk to them before the puppy arrives. Beagles are good dogs for children, but this will be the little dog's first time away from its mother, siblings, and familiar surroundings. The initial transition is important. Supervise all interactions for everyone's safety and comfort.

Help children understand how to handle the puppy and to carry it safely. Limit playtime until everyone gets to know each other. It won't be any time before your Beagle and your kids are running around all over the house and yard. You'll be amazed by just how hard it is to actually wear a Beagle out!

Introductions with Other Pets

Introductions with other dogs and even with cats often boil down to matters of territoriality. All dogs, by nature, defend their territory against intruders. Beagles have a strongly protective territorial urge and because they are hounds, they may chase cats.

Neither of these behaviors does anything to facilitate a peace agreement with Fluffy. It's always best in a multi-pet household to let the animals work out the order of dominance in the family "pack" on their own if possible. To begin this process, create a neutral and controlled interaction under a closed bathroom door first.

Since cats are "weaponized" with an array of razor sharp claws, they can quickly put a puppy in his place. A swipe to the nose won't do a puppy any harm, but don't let things get out of hand. Oversee the first "in person" meeting, but try not to overreact.

With other dogs in the house, you may want a more hands-on approach to the first "meet and greet." Always have two people present to control each dog. Make the introduction in a place that the older dog does not regard as "his." Even if the two dogs are going to be living in the same house, let them meet in neutral territory.

Keep your tone and demeanor calm, friendly, and happy. Let the dogs conduct the usual "sniff test," but don't let it go on for too long. Either dog may consider lengthy sniffing to be aggression.

Photo Credit: Sandra Groeschel of The Whim.

Puppies may not yet understand the behavior of an adult dog and can be absolute little pests. If the puppy does get too "familiar," do not scold the older dog for issuing a warning snarl or growl.

A well-socialized older dog won't be displaying aggression with this reaction. He's just putting junior in his place and establishing the hierarchy of the pack.

Be careful when you bring a new Beagle into the house not to neglect the older dog. Be sure to spend time with him away from the puppy to assure your existing pet that your bond with him is strong and intact.

Exercise caution at mealtimes. Feed your pets in separate bowls so there is no perceived competition for food. This is also a good policy to follow when introducing your puppy to the family cat.

What Can I Do to Make My Beagle Love Me?

From the moment you bring your Beagle dog home, every minute you spend with him is an opportunity to bond. Your Beagle has left the warmth and security of his mother and littermates, so initially for a few days he will be confused and even sad. It is important to make the transition from the birth home to your home as easy as possible.

The earlier you start working with your dog, the more quickly that bond will grow and the closer you and your Beagle will become. While simply spending time with your Beagle will encourage the growth of that bond, there are a few things you can do to purposefully build your bond with your dog. Some of these things include:

1. **Engaging** your Beagle in games like fetch and hide-and-seek to encourage interaction.

2. Taking your Beagle for **daily walks.** Frequently stop to pet and talk to your dog. Allow him time to sniff and smell during these walks. He is a hound and loves to explore new scents.

3. Interacting with your dog through **daily training sessions** — teach your dog to pay attention when you say his name.

4. Being calm and consistent when training your dog — always use **positive reinforcement** rather than punishment.

5. Beagles love it when you gently **stroke and massage** areas of their body, just avoid the paws, tail and backside. When his body relaxes and eyes close you know you've hit the right spots!

Common Mistakes to Avoid

Don't play the "hand" game, where you slide the puppy across the floor with your hands and they scramble to collect themselves and run back across the floor for another go. This sort of "game" will teach your puppy to disrespect you as their leader — first, because this "game" teaches them that humans are their play toys, and secondly, it teaches them that humans are a source of excitement. A Beagle is NOT a toy!

When your Beagle puppy is teething, they will naturally want to chew on everything within reach, and this will include you. As cute as you might think it is when they are young puppies, this is not an acceptable behavior, and you need to gently, but firmly, discourage the habit, just like a mother dog does to her puppies when they need to be weaned.

Always **praise your puppy** when they stop inappropriate behavior, as this starts to teach them to understand rules and boundaries. Often we humans are quick to discipline a puppy or dog for inappropriate behavior, but we forget to praise them for their good behavior.

Photo Credit: Ruth Darlene Stewart of Aladar Beagles.

Don't treat your Beagle like a small, furry human. When people **try to turn dogs into people**, this can cause them much stress and confusion that could lead to behavioral problems.

A well-behaved Beagle **thrives on rules and boundaries**, and when they understand that there is no question you are their leader and they are your follower, they will live a contented, happy, and stress-free life.

Dogs are a species with different rules from us; for example, they do not naturally cuddle, and they need to learn to be stroked and cuddled by humans. Be careful when approaching a dog for the first time and being overly expressive with your hands. The safest areas to touch are the back and chest — avoid patting on the head and touching the ears.

Many people will assume that a dog that is yawning is tired — this is often a misinterpretation, and instead the dog is signaling that he/she is not a threat.

Be careful when **staring at dogs** because this is one of the ways in which they threaten each other. This body language can make them feel distinctly uneasy.

Habituation and Socialization

Habituation is when you continuously provide exposure to the same stimuli over a period of time. This will help your Beagle to relax in his environment and will teach him how to behave around unfamiliar people, noises, other pets, and different surroundings. Expose your Beagle puppy continuously to new sounds and new environments.

When you allow for your Beagle to face life's positive experiences through socialization and habituation, you're helping your Beagle to build a library of valuable information that he can use when he's faced with a difficult situation. If he's had plenty of wonderful and positive early experiences, the more likely he'll be able to bounce back from any surprising or scary experiences.

When your Beagle puppy arrives at his new home for the first time, he'll start bonding with his human family immediately. This will be his **primary** bond. His **secondary** bond will be with everyone outside your home. A dog should never be secluded inside his home. Be sure to find the right balance, where you're not exposing your Beagle puppy to too much external stimuli.

If he starts becoming fearful, speak to your veterinarian. The puppyhood journey can be tiresome yet very rewarding. Primary socialization starts between three and five weeks of age, when a pup's experiences take place within his litter. This will have a huge impact on all his future emotional behavior.

Socialization from six to twelve weeks allows for puppies to bond with other species outside of their littermates and parents. It's at this stage that most pet parents will bring home a puppy and where he'll soon become comfortable with humans, other pets, and children.

By the time a puppy is around twelve to fourteen weeks, he becomes more difficult to introduce to new environments and new people and starts showing suspicion and distress. Nonetheless, if you've recently bought a Beagle puppy or are bringing one home and he's beyond this ideal age, don't neglect to continue the socialization process. Puppies need to be exposed to as many new situations, environments, people, and other animals as possible, and **it is never too late to start**.

During puppyhood, you can easily teach your puppy to politely greet a new person, yet by the time a puppy has reached social maturity, the same puppy, if not properly socialized, may start lunging forward and acting aggressively, with the final outcome of lunging and nipping.

Never accidentally reward your Beagle puppy for displaying fear or growling at another dog or animal by picking them up. Picking up a Beagle puppy or dog at this time, when they are displaying unbalanced energy, actually turns out **to be a reward for them**, and you will be teaching them to continue with this type of behavior. As well, picking up a puppy literally places them in a "top dog" position where they are higher and more dominant than the dog or animal they just growled at.

If they are doing something you do not want them to continue, your puppy needs to be gently corrected by you with firm and calm energy, so that they learn not to react with fear or aggression. When the mum of the litter tells her puppies off, she will use a deep noise with strong eye contact, until the puppy quickly realizes it's doing something naughty.

The same is true of situations where a young puppy may feel the need to protect themselves from a bigger or older dog that may come charging in for a sniff. It is the guardian's responsibility to protect the puppy so that they do not think they must react with fear or aggression in order to protect themselves.

Once your Beagle puppy has received all their vaccinations, you can take them out to public dog parks and various locations where many dogs are found. Before allowing them to interact with other dogs or puppies, take them for a disciplined walk on leash so that they will be a little tired and less likely to immediately engage with all other dogs.

Keep your puppy on leash and close beside you, because most puppies are usually a bundle of out-of-control energy, and **you need to protect them** while teaching them how far they can go before getting themselves into trouble with adult dogs who may not appreciate excited puppy playfulness.

If your Beagle puppy shows any signs of aggression or domination toward another dog, **immediately step in** and calmly discipline them.

Photo Credit: Susie Arden of Madika Beagles.

Look out for initial warning signs that indicate a buildup of aggression, which could escalate between two dogs: biting of lip, backing away, crouching, growling, fearful posture, tail tucking, snapping, and lunging.

Stopping a Fight

Most owners will instinctually scream loudly at the dogs, but this rarely has an effect and can even cause it to get more out of hand! Stepping into the middle of two fighting dogs can be extremely dangerous and could easily result in physical harm. Here are some tips:

1. Most fights will appear worse than they really are even if there is a lot of noise and motion going on. If there is biting it is usually a quick "bite and then release."

2. Avoid grabbing the head or neck area of either dog with your hands.

3. Place your foot on the rib cage of one of them and push him away.

4. Pull them apart by grabbing their rear ends.

5. Distract them by spraying the dogs with water.

6. Get some object such as an item of your clothing (e.g., your coat) between them or over them.

7. Be careful that the offending dog(s) do not turn their aggression towards you!

Take your Beagle puppy everywhere with you and introduce them to different people of all ages, sizes, and ethnicities. Most people will come to you and want to interact with your puppy. If they ask if they can hold your puppy, let them, as long as they are gentle. This is a good way to socialize your Beagle and show them that humans are friendly.

As important as socialization is, it is also important that your Beagle be **left alone for short periods** when young so that they can cope with some periods of isolation. If an owner goes out and they have never experienced this, they can destroy things or make a mess because of panic. They are thinking they are vulnerable and can be attacked by something or someone coming into the house.

Safety First

Never think for a minute that your Beagle would not bolt and run away. Even well-adjusted, happy puppies and adult dogs can run away, usually in extreme conditions such as during fireworks, thunder, or when scared.

If he gets lost, it is important he can be identified:

1. Get him a collar with an ID tag because some people may presume that dogs without collars have been abandoned. Note that hanging tags can get caught on things.

2. Put your phone number but not his name on the tag in case he is stolen. A thief will then not be able to use his name. Consider saying, "for reward, call."

3. Inserting a microchip below the skin via injection is recommended, as this cannot be removed easily by a thief.

4. Recent photos of your Beagle need to be placed in your wallet or purse.

Train your Beagle — foster and work with a professional, positive trainer to ensure that your dog does not run out the front door or out the backyard gate. Teach your Beagle basic, simple commands such as "come" and "stay."

Create a special, fun digging area just for him, hide his bones and toys, and let your Beagle know that it's okay to dig in that area. After all, dogs need to play!

Introduce your new, furry companion to all your neighbors, so everyone will know that he belongs to you.

Know that your Beagle will not instinctively be fearful of cars, so be very careful around roads.

Chapter 6 — Beagle Housetraining

This section covers the all-important training of your Beagle to go relieve themselves outside. This is referred to as housebreaking or housetraining, and in America it is often referred to as **potty training**.

When the Beagle is born, they relieve themselves inside their den, with the mother cleaning them up so there is never a scent of urine or feces where the puppies eat, sleep, and live. As they get older, they follow their mother's lead in learning to go outside, so housetraining may already be established by your breeder when you take your puppy home. If not, they are probably well on the way already. They just need some extra guidance from you.

Photo Credit: Stacey Burrows of Summerlily Beagles.

New owners always ask me how long it will take — there is no timetable for a dog being totally housetrained. Yes, it can be as quick as two weeks, but each pup is an individual and some pick up faster than others. Patience, being consistent in taking them out, and praise when they go are the keys to success. Also, take note on the times the pup needs to go out. This is helpful with taking them out on their schedule.

Joan Wurst of Everwind Beagles: "While I do not dispute the fact that some Beagles may be difficult to housebreak (due to their strong-willed nature), in my personal experience (and that of many of my puppy buyers) I have not found them exceptionally hard to housebreak. My youngest one began housebreaking herself at 5 weeks, as long as I paid enough attention to her to recognize her hints. She was extremely easy and I can honestly say I've not had a hard one."

Carol Herr of Roirdan Beagles says: "They are so food motivated, you can teach them most anything BUT, and it is a big BUT, you have to be consistent. I crate train all my dogs. As soon as I get up in the morning, they come out of their crate and go outside. Usually as soon as they hit the ground they have to go. They get tons of praise and a cookie. It only takes a short time and I discontinue the cookies and they only get praise. You also have to have patience. In the house I watch VERY closely. When they start to circle and get anxious, I pick them out."

We have already stressed the importance of being at home for the first two weeks (at least) when you bring your pup back from the breeder. If he is left on his own, expect him to eliminate inside the house because at this stage he doesn't realize that the whole house is in effect his den and not the place to eliminate.

Crate training and housebreaking go hand in hand. Beagles, like all dogs, come to **see their crate as their den**. They will hold their need to urinate or defecate while they are inside.

Establishing and maintaining a daily routine also helps your dog in this respect. Feed your Beagle at the same time each day, taking him out afterwards. The feeding schedule dictates the frequency of "relief" breaks. Trips out will also decrease as the dog ages.

Don't be rigid in holding your puppy to this standard. Puppies have less control over their bladder and bowel movements than adult Beagles. They need to go out more often, especially after they've been active or have become excited.

On average, adult dogs go **out 3–4 times a day**: when they wake up, within an hour of eating, and right before bedtime. With puppies, don't wait more than 15 minutes after a meal.

If you are keeping your Beagle puppy in a crate overnight, he will need to be let out once or twice a night, as he will not be able to hold it in the whole night until he is aged about four or five months old.

Getting your Beagle puppy to go outside from day one is best. Your Beagle will want to keep eliminating in the same spot because the scent acts as **a signal 'to go'** in their mind. In time this spot becomes safe and familiar to them. Don't allow them to go on your lawn; being soft, they like this because it feels good under their paws. A discreet corner furthest away from your back door is best, perhaps an area of gravel or, if you live in an apartment, you can use a dog litter tray.

Praise your Beagle with the same phrases to encourage and reinforce good elimination habits. NEVER punish him for having an accident. There is no association in his mind with the punishment and the incident. He'll have an uncomfortable awareness that he's done *something* to make you unhappy, but **he won't know what.**

Getting upset or scolding a puppy for having an accident inside the home is the wrong approach, because this will result in teaching your puppy to be afraid of you and to only relieve themselves in secret places or when you're not watching.

If you catch your Beagle puppy making a mistake, calmly say "no," and take them outside or to their indoor bathroom area. Resist the temptation to scoop him up, because he needs to learn to walk to the door himself when he needs to go outside.

Clean up the accident using an enzymatic cleaner to eradicate the odor and return to the dog's normal routine. Nature's Miracle Stain and Odor Removal is an excellent product and affordable at $5 / £2.97 per 32-ounce / 0.9-liter bottle.

Sharon Hardisty of Blunderhall Beagles recommends: "Simple Solutions Stain + Odour Remover, an enzyme cleaner £18.99 for 4 litres, £4.99 for 1 litre."

I'm not a big fan of puppy pads because I find puppies like the softness of the pads, which can encourage them to eliminate on other soft areas — such as your carpets!

Check in with yourself and make sure your energy remains consistently calm and patient, and that you exercise plenty of compassion and understanding while you help your new puppy learn the bathroom rules. Don't clean up after your puppy with them watching, as this makes the puppy believe you are there to clean up after them, making you lower in the dog pack order.

While your Beagle is still growing, on average, they can hold it approximately one hour for every month of their age. This means that if your 3-month-old puppy has been happily snoozing for two to three hours, as soon as they wake up, they will need to go outside.

Some of the first indications or signs that your puppy needs to be taken outside to relieve themselves will be when you see them:

• Sniffing around
• Circling
• Looking for the door
• Whining, crying, or barking
• Acting agitated

During the early stages of potty training, adding treats as an extra incentive can be a good way to reinforce how happy you are that your puppy is learning to relieve themselves in the right place. Slowly, treats can be removed and replaced with your happy praise, or you can give your puppy a treat after they are back inside.

Next, now that you have a new puppy in your life, you will want to be flexible with respect to adapting your schedule to meet their internal clocks to quickly teach your Beagle puppy their new bathroom routine.

This means not leaving your puppy alone for endless hours at a time, because firstly, they are pack animals that need companionship and your direction at all times, plus long periods alone will result in the disruption of the potty training schedule you have worked so hard to establish.

If you have no choice but to leave your puppy alone for many hours, make sure that you place them in a paper-lined room or pen where they can relieve themselves without destroying your newly installed hardwood or favorite carpet. Remember, your Beagle is a growing puppy with a bladder and bowels that they do not yet have complete control over.

Bell Training

A very easy way to introduce your new Beagle puppy to house training is to begin by teaching them how to ring a bell whenever they need to go outside. A further benefit of training your puppy to ring a bell is that you will not have to listen to your puppy or dog whining, barking, or howling to be let out, and your door will not become scratched up from their nails.

Attach several bells to a piece of ribbon or string and hang it from a door handle, or tape it to a doorsill near the door where you will be taking your puppy out when they need to relieve themselves. The string will need to be long enough so that your puppy can easily reach the bell with their nose or a paw.

Next, each time you take your puppy out to relieve themselves, say the word "out," and use their paw or their nose to ring the bell. Praise them for this "trick" and immediately take them outside. This type of an alert system is an easy way to eliminate accidents in the home.

Kennel Training

When you train your Beagle puppy to accept sleeping in their own kennel at nighttime, this will also help to accelerate their potty training. Because no puppy or dog wants to relieve themselves where they sleep, they will hold their bladder and bowels as long as they possibly can.

Presenting them with familiar scents by taking them to the same spot in the yard or the same street corner will help to remind and encourage them that they are outside to relieve themselves.

Use a voice cue to remind your puppy why they are outside, such as "go pee," and always praise them each time they relieve themselves in the right place, so that they quickly understand what you expect of them.

Exercise Pen Training

The exercise pen is a transition from kennel-only training and will be helpful for those times when you may have to leave your Beagle puppy for more hours than they can reasonably be expected to hold it, although we repeat that many of our breeders don't think any dog should be left for more than four hours at a stretch.

Exercise pens are usually constructed of wire sections that you can put together in whatever shape you desire, and the pen needs to be large enough to hold your puppy's kennel in one half of the pen, while the

other half will be lined with newspapers, pee pads, or a potty pan with pellets.

Place your Beagle puppy's food and water dishes next to the kennel and leave the kennel door open (or take it off), so they can wander in and out whenever they wish to eat or drink or go to the papers, pan, or pee pads if they need to relieve themselves.

Because they are already used to sleeping inside their kennel, they will not want to relieve themselves inside the area where they sleep. Therefore, your puppy will naturally go to the other half of the pen to relieve themselves.

Accelerated Potty Training

This is my advanced, highly detailed guide to housetraining your Beagle. This is what I recommend for the first four weeks of potty training; after that this needs to be continued but the owner can now give them more freedom.

What I describe below has to be interspersed with exercise and play time of a good intensity — at least every few hours. If puppies do not  get this freedom to expend their puppy/high energy, they will at the end of the day be prone to aggressive behavior, including biting and nipping to try and get their energy out! This develops into a dangerous pattern. As a matter of fact, during training I wake up the puppies and do not let them nap any longer than 45 minutes at a time — this will help the puppy expend that pent-up energy all day long.

1. Upon wake up, about 5:30 a.m., even before humans use the bathroom, take your puppy out of the closed crate, scooping him up quickly and taking a leash with you. Once he hears you walking about, he will have to "go." Go to a designated outdoor spot and use the same spot for the next few weeks. Put the leash on (I use a leash with a loop at the end because at this age, the puppy gets his skin irritated with a regular collar and is very distracted by this.) When you come back in, set the alarm for an hourly schedule. Everything is from the perspective of planning for this hour.

2. Day one will be different than all other days. Please do not use any command when you get outside. Instead, put the puppy down on the ground and wait. He will eliminate. As he is eliminating say the command: "go potty" (this is what I use, it should be a short command).

3. Continue this method all day for the first day. If you do not do it this way, your puppy will have no idea what any command means. You have to say the command while you "catch him" eliminating. Do this many times. Immediately "mark" the behavior with a praise phrase and give a sliver of a treat simultaneously. No treats in the house, just for potty training. Exceptions are chew treats, veggies, fruits, nothing with caloric content.

4. Day two, you can start giving the command prior to his eliminating.

5. So after the wake-up trip outside, if your puppy does nothing, back in the crate for 10 minutes (door closed), then outside again. Keep repeating this every 10 minutes until he goes.

6. If you puppy does both urine and bowel movement, and after the treat reward and praise — which must be instantaneous — bring him in. He is again rewarded with complete freedom for 10 minutes. After 10 minutes, he is still rewarded with "limited freedom" for another 10–15 minutes inside the exercise pen. If your puppy only does one — either urine or bowel movement but not both, bring him in and he goes straight to the exercise pen only for 10 minutes. He does not get complete freedom; he gets limited freedom. During these freedom and limited freedom times, you will want to, several times a day, get into the pen and play very actively with him, and interact with toys as well.

7. After this "reward" time, puppy goes back into the crate, door shut. He stays in crate until that specific hour is up, unless it is breakfast, lunch, or dinner time. Then you start the whole process again.

8. For purposes of potty training, instead of putting him back in the crate for the whole hour, you can hold your puppy as long as you want. You can also let him play outside during this time. Puppies will not eliminate while being held; puppies will eliminate while playing outside but that is ok. This will help you to help him stay awake and expend more of that puppy energy.

9. If it is the first "take out" trip for the day, after your pup has eliminated and while still in the pen, feed him breakfast. Give him 10 minutes to eat, then remove food. Put him back in the crate after he takes his last bite, have him stay in the crate and after 10 minutes, start the potty routine again. After your puppy eats is one of those times that you must take him out again because digestion has started and moves along quickly; he will have to go again about 10 minutes after eating.

10. So the times that you start the "go potty" trip outside are:

- First thing in the morning
- 10 minutes after each meal

- Immediately upon wake up from a nap (and we do not let them sleep for very long periods, as you will have a puppy who has been crated too many hours during the day and will have anxiety at the end of the day)
- Last thing at the end of the day, as late as possible: 10 p.m. or 11 p.m.
- For the first two weeks, every 4 hours at night or if the puppy cries in the crate
- Keep the hourly schedule for the most part

11. At the four-week mark, you can start expanding the freedom and limited freedom times. You will learn what is best for your puppy.

This method has some "secret" tips that are critical. For example, on day one, it's best not to give any command outside to potty. The pup will have no idea what the person is talking about. Bring puppy out first thing in the morning and just WAIT. Once the puppy starts a bowel movement or starts to urinate, say the command, whatever it is.

Do this for all of day one. If you don't, he won't make the connection very quickly, it will be much slower; I truly believe my pups are 85% of the way after 2 weeks. Even on the third day, they have made the connection between the command and what we want from it.

Families who follow this training schedule report zero accidents or very few, which they always attribute to their own mistakes. This method works and if you can put in the initial time, you won't have to worry about struggling with potty training for months and months.

I also find that our Beagles never cry in the middle of the night unless they truly have to pee or poop. And this is usually limited to the first two weeks; when they whine at 2 a.m. you can be sure it is because they have to go potty. Puppies who cry in the middle of the night for other reasons may not yet be confident about the whole training system. The first two weeks we make a point of taking them out about 2 a.m.; then after that, there will be no need. Occasionally they will whine in the middle of the night and definitely have to go depending upon whether their bladder and intestines were emptied out by 10 p.m. or not and how late they ate or drank.

Marking Territory

Both male and female dogs with intact reproductive systems mark territory by urinating. This is most often an outdoor behavior, but can happen inside if the dog is upset. Again, use an enzymatic cleaner to

remove the odor and minimize the attractiveness of the location to the dog. Territory marking is especially prevalent in intact males. The obvious long-term solution is to have the dog neutered.

Photo Credit: Claudia Anderson of TwainHeart Beagles.

Marking territory is not a consequence of poor housetraining. The behavior can be seen in dogs that would otherwise never "go" in the house. It stems from completely different urges and reactions.

Edy Ballard of Ironwood Beagles: "I have found some female Beagles to be especially stubborn when it comes to housetraining, and I have some (females) that are chronic markers. My females have been far worse than my males. This usually occurs when there are multiple dogs in a home and the Beagle wants to mark off 'her' bed, corner, etc. In my experience, the Beagle girls are much harder to housetrain and can take much patience before they get it right."

Dealing with Separation Anxiety

Separation anxiety manifests in a variety of ways, ranging from vocalizations to nervous chewing. Dogs that are otherwise well-trained may urinate or defecate in the house. These behaviors begin when your dog recognizes **signs that you are leaving**. Triggers include picking up a set of car keys or putting on a coat. The dog may start to follow you around the house trying to get your attention, jumping up on you or otherwise trying to touch you.

It is imperative that you understand when you take on a Beagle that **they are companion dogs**. They must have time to connect and be with their humans. You are the center of your dog's world. The behavior that a dog exhibits when it has separation anxiety is not a case of the animal being "bad." The poor thing experiences real distress and loneliness.

Being with him most of the time can cause him to be over-reliant on you, and then he will get stressed when left alone. As discussed earlier, it is wise to leave him on his own for a few minutes every day so he understands this is normal. You can increase this time gradually.

Remember that to a new puppy, you have now **taken the place of his mother and littermates**. He is completely reliant on you, so it is natural for him to follow you everywhere initially.

As well as puppies, you may also see separation anxiety in rescued dogs and senior (older) dogs.

13 Tips for Leaving Your Beagle During the Daytime

Your Beagle loves to be with you and they are very much in tune to recognizing those situations where you are going to leave them. They will go through a myriad of antics to avoid being left alone. Being realistic, most of us have to go to work. While we recommend you take a couple of weeks off when you get your new puppy, the time will come to go back to work during the day.

1. Get a neighbor or friend to come in around lunchtime to spend some time with your Beagle.

2. Employ a dog walker or come home yourself during your lunch break and take him for a walk.

3. Is there anyone, family, friends, etc. you could leave him with?

4. Exercise generates serotonin in the brain and has a calming effect. Walk him before your work and he will be less anxious and more ready for a good nap.

5. Leave some toys lying around for playtime to prevent boredom and destructive behaviors such as chewing and barking. Many toys can be filled with tasty treats that should do the trick!

6. Make sure that the temperature is moderate. You don't want your dog getting too cold or too hot in the place where you leave him.

7. Don't leave food down all day — he may become a fussy eater. Set specific meal times and remove it after 15–20 minutes if uneaten. This doesn't apply to water — make sure he has access to water at all times.

8. Leave him where he feels most comfortable. Near his crate with the door open is a good option.

9. Play some soothing music on repeat. There are dog-specific audio tracks that claim to ease separation anxiety. Often a dog will become concerned in a totally quiet environment and that may amplify their anxiety.

10. Stick to the same routine each day. Don't overly fuss him before you leave OR when you return. Keep it low key and normal.

11. Do your leaving routine such as putting shoes on, getting car keys, etc. and go out and come back almost immediately to build this experience into their brain gradually. Steadily increase the length over time. Do this almost as soon as your puppy comes home, so it won't be such a shock to him when you really do need to leave him alone.

12. Make sure other family members do things with your Beagle, e.g., feeding, walking, playing, so he doesn't become over reliant on you.

13. Never punish him. They may do some bad things, but this is not their fault and they do not mean to be bad on purpose. You WILL make the situation even worse if you do this.

Chapter 7 — Food & Exercise

This is perhaps the most important chapter in the book because whatever you feed your Beagle **affects the length and quality of his life**. Remember too that they are driven by food so will eat pretty much anything put in front of them; and they will eat as much as they can, so it is down to you as to what type of food they eat and how much.

Do not free feed (leave food out at all times) with a Beagle! They are superior beggars and because the breed is often under-exercised, the combination of these two factors can lead to rapid obesity.

When it comes to what food to serve to your precious Beagle, the choices seem endless. There is **no one best food** because some dogs need higher fat and protein than others, and some prefer canned over dry.

While food manufacturers are out to maximize their profits, as a rule you usually get what you pay for. So a more expensive food is generally more likely to provide **better nutrition** for your Beagle in terms of minerals, nutrients, and higher quality meats in comparison to a cheap one, which will most likely **contain a lot of grain**. Even today, far too many dog food choices continue to have far more to do with being convenient for us humans to serve than they do with being a well-balanced, healthy food choice.

We will help guide you through the maze of the supermarket shelves, but in order to choose the right food for your Beagle, first it's important to understand a little bit about canine physiology and what Mother Nature intended when she created our furry companions.

While humans are omnivores who can derive energy from eating plants, our canine companions are **natural carnivores**, which means they derive their energy and nutrient requirements from eating a diet consisting mainly or exclusively of the flesh of animals, birds, or fish — this provides proteins. Yes, proteins can be obtained from non-meat sources, but these are generally harder for the body to digest and have a higher chance of causing dietary intolerances.

Although dogs **can survive** on an omnivorous diet, this **does not mean** it is the best diet for them. Unlike humans, who are equipped with wide, flat molars for grinding grains, vegetables, and other plant-based materials, canine teeth are all pointed because they are designed to rip, shred, and tear into meat and bone.

Dogs are also born equipped with powerful jaws and neck muscles for the specific purpose of being able to pull down and tear apart their hunted prey. The structure of the jaw of every canine is such that it opens widely to hold large pieces of meat and bone, while the mechanics of a dog's jaw permits only vertical (up and down) movement that is designed for crushing.

The Canine Digestive Tract

A dog's digestive tract is short and simple and designed to move their natural choice of food (hide, meat, and bone) quickly through their system. Given the choice, most dogs would **never choose** to eat plants and grains, or vegetables and fruits over meat, however, we humans continue to feed them a kibble-based diet that contains high amounts of vegetables, fruits, and grains with low amounts of meat. Part of this is because we've been taught that it's a healthy, balanced diet for humans, and therefore, we believe that it must be the same for our dogs, and part of this is because all the fillers that make up our dog's food are less expensive and easier to process than meat.

While dogs can eat omnivorous foods, we are simply suggesting the **majority of their diet should consist of meats**.

One of the questions dog owners often ask is "Do dogs need fruits and vegetables?" In a 2006 committee on Animal Nutrition, the NRC confirmed dogs have **no nutritional requirements for carbohydrates**.

In their 2010 Pet Food Nutrient Profiles, the AAFCO concluded **carbohydrates are not essential to a healthy canine diet**.

But can plants play a role in supplementation? Many believe that **yes, plants can be a healthful addition** to the modern dog's diet and that vegetables provide essential nutrients, including fiber, minerals, and vitamins that an all-meat diet lacks. Advocates note that modern, intensive agricultural methods have stripped increasing amounts of nutrients from the soil. Crops grown decades ago (and the animals that ate them) were much richer in vitamins, minerals, and other nutrients than most of the varieties we get today.

Whatever you decide to feed your dog, keep in mind that just as too much wheat, other grains, and fillers in our human diet is having a detrimental effect on our health, the same can be very true for our best fur friends. Our dogs are also suffering from many of the same life-threatening diseases that are rampant in our **human society** as a direct result of consuming a diet high in genetically altered, impure, processed, and packaged foods.

Top Feeding Tips

High-quality dog foods provide all the nutrients, vitamins, minerals, and calories that your dog needs. This makes it a lot easier than our human diet where we have to make sure we eat many varieties of foods, and even then, we may be deficient in an important mineral or vitamin. But a word of warning: just because a food is branded as "premium" **doesn't mean it is**. The word is meaningless marketing.

Before buying any dog food, read the label. The first (main ingredient by weight) listed ingredients **should be a meat** such as beef, chicken, lamb, or fish.

Foods with large amounts of fillers like cornmeal or meat by-products have a **low nutritional value**. They fill your dog up, but don't give him the necessary range of vitamins and minerals, and they increase daily waste produced.

If grains are used, look for **whole grains** (i.e., whole grain corn, whole grain barley) and not cheaper by-products (corn gluten meal, soybean meal).

High-end premium diets avoid grains altogether in favor of carbohydrates such as white or sweet potato.

Avoid artificial colors like Erythrosine, also known as Red No. 3, preservatives such as BHA, BHT, Ethoxyquin, and sweeteners such as sucrose or high fructose corn syrup. Cut out sugars and salt.

AAFCO stands for the Association of American Feed Control Officials. They develop guidelines for the production, labeling, and sale of animal foods. Choose a diet that complies with AAFCO specifications and conducts feeding trials. The label will say: Animal feeding tests using AAFCO procedures substantiate that (name of product) provides complete and balanced nutrition.

Grain free (or raw) is often recommended for the Beagle. Many are **allergic** to corn starch, wheat, and some other grains. In addition, no soy should be in the dog food — it irritates them!

Wet foods are not appropriate for most growing dogs. They do not offer a good nutritional balance, and they are often upsetting to the stomach. Additionally, it's much harder to control portions with wet food, leading to young dogs being overfed or underfed.

If your Beagle does not eat all of its meal in one go, you may be offering it too much. Many owners ask how many times a day they should feed, and the reality is it doesn't matter — what does is the correct feeding amount. You then divide this up by the number of meals you wish to serve. Most owners opt for twice a day for adult dogs.

Stools should be firm, dark brown, and crinkly if portions are correct — if firm but softer towards the end, this is an indication of overfeeding. Stools are an **indicator** of digestive upsets, if you notice they are runny or hard, there is a problem, as is excessive wind or an abnormal amount of feces. These should also not be brightly colored or smelly. Mucous in the stool is a common symptom of irritable bowel syndrome (IBS).

Invest in weighted food and water bowls made out of **stainless steel**. The weights prevent the mess of "tip overs," and the material is much easier to clean than plastic. It does not hold odors or harbor bacteria.

Bowls in a stand that create an **elevated feeding surface** are also a good idea. Make sure your young dog can reach the food and water. Stainless steel bowl sets retail for less than $25 / £14.87.

Leave your Beagle **alone** while it is eating from its bowl. Don't take the bowl away while he is eating. This causes anxiety, which can lead to **food aggression.**

Do you have more than one dog? I advise **feeding them separately** to completely avoid potential issues. One might try protecting his own food aggressively or try to eat the food designated for the other dog.

Feeding Your Puppy

As Beagles age, they thrive on a graduated program of nutrition. Up to the age of four months, puppies should get **four small meals** a day. From age 4–8 months, **three meals** per day are appropriate. From 8 months on, feed your Beagle **twice** a day and consider switching to an adult formula.

TIP: From the very beginning of weaning, I put my hands into the puppies' bowls and feed them from my hands. I will take the food bowl from them and immediately offer them a tasty treat, then return their bowl. All of this teaches the puppy it is okay for hands to be around their food. I feel this is a very important life lesson where children are involved. Also, if a puppy grabs something that is not safe for them, they are much more willing to relinquish it.

Beagles will eat pretty much anything and everything put in front of them, so it is up to you to control their portions!

I highly recommend feeding puppies and dogs in the crate/kennel.

Begin feeding your puppy by putting the food down for 10–20 minutes. If the dog doesn't eat, or only eats part of the serving, still **take the bowl up**. Don't give the dog more until the next feeding time.

Scheduled feedings in measured amounts are the preferred option and are less likely to lead to a fussy eater.

To give your puppy a good start in life, rely on high-quality, premium dry puppy food. If possible, replicate the puppy's existing diet. A sudden **dietary switch** can cause gastrointestinal upset, as puppies have sensitive stomachs. Take your pup to the vet if he has diarrhea or he has been vomiting for 48 hours or more.

Maintain the dog's existing routine if practical. To make an effective food transition, mix the existing diet with the new food, slowly changing the percentage of new to old over a period of 10 days.

Some breeders recommend not using puppy food. It can be high in protein and actually can cause the puppy to **grow too fast**, thus possibly creating bone growth issues. You may want to switch to a junior or adult food once he leaves puppyhood. Your vet will help decide when best to switch.

Adult Nutrition

The same basic nutritional guidelines apply to adult Beagles. Always start with a high-quality, premium food. If possible, stay in the same product line the puppy received at the breeder. Graduated product lines help owners to create feeding programs that ensure nutritional consistency. This approach allows you to transition your Beagle away from puppy food to an adult mixture, and in time, to a senior formula. This removes the guesswork from nutritional management.

Beagles should be fed **at least** twice a day to avoid bloat, which can be fatal. You should also **avoid exercise** immediately before or after eating.

Dogs don't make it easy to say no when they beg at the table. If you let a Beagle puppy have so much as that first bite, you've created a little monster — and one with an unhealthy habit. As well as begging, this encourages drooling and negative attention-seeking behavior such as barking.

Never Feed These to Your Beagle

Table scraps contribute to weight problems, and many human foods are toxic to dogs. They may be too rich for your Beagle and cause him to scratch. Dangerous (some potentially fatal) items include:

- Chocolate
- Raisins and grapes
- Alcohol
- Human vitamins (especially those with iron)
- Mushrooms
- Garlic
- Onions
- Walnuts
- Macadamia nuts

Also, avoid sausage meat and cooked manufactured meats, as they can contain sulphite preservatives that can be harmful.

Never feed your Beagle **cooked bones**, as these can splinter and cause internal damage or become an intestinal obstruction. If you give your puppy a bone, watch him. Use only bones that are too large to choke on and take the item away at the first sign of splintering. Commercial chew toys rated "puppy safe" are a much better option.

The Dehydrated Diet (Freeze-Dried)

Dehydrated dog food comes in both raw and cooked forms, and these foods are usually air-dried to reduce moisture to the level where bacterial growth is inhibited.

The appearance of dehydrated dog food is very similar to dry kibble, and the typical feeding methods include adding warm water before serving, which makes this type of diet both healthy for our dogs and convenient for us to serve.

Dehydrated recipes are made from minimally-processed fresh whole foods to create a healthy and nutritionally balanced meal that will meet or exceed the dietary requirements for healthy canines.

Dehydrating removes only the moisture from the fresh ingredients, which usually means that because the food has not already been cooked at a high temperature, more of the overall nutrition is retained.

A dehydrated diet is a convenient way to feed your dog a nutritious diet, because all you have to do is add warm water and wait five minutes while the food rehydrates so your Beagle can enjoy a warm meal. There are, however, some potential disadvantages. It is **more expensive** than other diets (you are paying for the convenience factor), and because of the processing it can also **contain more preservatives** than you might ideally want.

Kibble Diet or Canned Food?

While many canine guardians are starting to take a closer look at the food choices they are making for their furry companions, there is no mistaking that the convenience and relative economy of dry dog food kibble, which had its beginnings in the 1940s, continues to make it the most popular dog food choice for most humans. It is basically one of the least expensive choices and is quick, easy, and convenient to serve.

Dry kibble dog food is less messy than canned, easier to measure, and can sit out all day without going bad. It is more economical per pound and is more energy-dense than canned food. This is because dry food is usually only 10% water, compared with about 75% water in cans. It

takes a much larger volume of canned food to supply the nutrients your dog needs, as a can effectively only has 25% food. You are also likely to have to put half-finished cans in your fridge to keep them from going off, and they cause a strong smell which is unpleasant to some.

Be wary of cheap kibble, which often has high grain content and **is a false economy**, as they have to eat a lot to be well-nourished. Critics suggest that there is a lot of undercooked starch in a dry dog food that can lead to gut problems: wind, loose stools, itchy skin, and fungal problems.

Canned food diets do have some **advantages**. Food manufacturers artificially boost the taste appeal of dry kibble by coating it with tempting fats, gravy, and other flavorings. In comparison, the wet and moist food fresh out of a can is much more edible to your Beagle and often contains more protein, fat, and less additives and preservatives. The texture and smell also have added appeal to their senses!

The BARF/Raw Diet

Raw feeding advocates believe that the ideal diet for their dog is one that would be very similar to what a dog living in the wild would have access to, and these canine guardians are often opposed to feeding their dog any sort of commercially manufactured pet foods.

On the other hand, those opposed to feeding their dogs a raw or Biologically Appropriate Raw Food (BARF) diet believe that the risks associated with food-borne illnesses during the handling and feeding of raw meats outweigh the purported benefits.

A typical BARF diet is made up of 60–80% of raw meaty bones (RMB). This is bones with about 50% meat, (e.g., chicken neck, back, and wings) and 20–40% of fruit and vegetables, offal, meat, eggs, or dairy foods.

Many owners directly oversee the raw diets, which usually consist of raw meat and bones, with some vegetables, fruits, supplements, and added grains.

Alternatively, you can buy commercial raw diet meals, which come either fresh or frozen. These supply all of the dog's requirements and are usually in a meat patty form. Always defrost it in the fridge, use what you need, and store the remainder on the bottom shelf of the fridge to use at the next mealtime, for up to four days.

Avoid feeding pork to your dog — eating raw or undercooked pork is not safe for dogs or humans due to the parasite Trichinella spiralis larvae, which can cause the trichinosis infection. Even if cooked, pork is rich with a type of fat that is difficult for them to digest, which can lead to indigestion and inflammation of the pancreas.

It is recommended that beef should be frozen before feeding, because of the Neospora intestinal parasite which can be found in cattle.

Many owners and breeders agree that their dogs thrive on a raw or BARF diet and strongly believe that the potential benefits of feeding a dog a raw food diet are many, including:

- Healthy, shiny coats
- Decreased shedding
- Fewer allergy problems
- Healthier skin
- Cleaner teeth
- Fresher breath
- Higher energy levels
- Improved digestion
- Smaller stools
- Strengthened immune system
- Increased mobility in arthritic pets
- General increase or improvement in overall health
- Ability to control what is in your Beagle's food bowl
- Ability to avoid ingredients they are allergic or intolerant to
- No preservatives or additives

All dogs, whether working breed or lap dogs, are amazing athletes in their own right and deserve to be fed the best food available. A raw diet is a direct evolution of what dogs ate before they became our domesticated pets and we turned toward commercially prepared, easy-to-serve dry dog food that required no special storage or preparation.

Many owners have reported seeing dogs plagued by chronic conditions such as atopy, obesity, and allergies, regaining their health after making the switch over to raw. The diet is low in carbs and free from grains, which turn directly into sugar in the body leading to fat deposition, and high in protein and fat.

A balanced raw diet naturally contains everything your dog could need nutritionally in an easily absorbable natural form. This means they won't seek out other food because of a deficiency. In addition, it also keeps them occupied for longer, so they are more likely to realize they're sated, and as they chew bones or chunks of meat, endorphins are released making them feel happier.

This all sounds good, doesn't it? So what **are the possible downsides?**

- Can be time consuming — less convenient.
- More expensive than other diets.
- Diet may not be balanced unless you are very careful — your Beagle may become deficient in minerals and vitamins.
- Raw vegetables are often poorly digested by dogs.
- Safety for the elderly and young children — raw diets have been found to contain Salmonella, Campylobacter, E. coli, Clostridium perfringens, Clostridium botulinium, and Staphylococcus aureus. These are all known human and canine pathogens.
- Safety to your Beagle — some raw foods contain pathogens which can make your dog very sick (even fatally) such as Neospora caninum, found in raw beef, Nanophyetus salmincola, found in raw salmon, and Trichinella spiralis, found in raw pork.

Raw food advocates simply suggest that you use common-sense practices such as washing your hands after handling raw food and cleaning your knives, chopping boards, and surfaces, either in the dishwasher or in hot soapy water. You can also put your dog's bowl in the dishwasher, which will kill bacteria.

If you can't feed your dog a raw diet for whatever reason, please think enough of him/her to at least feed a topical enzyme/probiotic so they can process their food better. These can help your dog with weight loss because a healthy gut means healthy digestion. Some naturally probiotic-rich foods are sauerkraut, kimchi, kefir, and live yoghurt (goat or sheep dairy is always better than cow).

TIP: Add some Psyllium Husk Fibre to the raw food. This expands in the stomach, leaving your Beagle feeling fuller and acts as a prebiotic. Not to be confused with probiotics, **prebiotics** stimulate the growth of friendly bacteria in the large intestine.

TIP: Organ tissues such as beef and bison liver provide essential amino acids necessary to supply your Beagle's high protein needs. Liver is one of the most nutrient-rich foods containing vitamin A, all B vitamins, D, and important minerals such as iron, phosphorus, and copper.

Veronica and Rosie Longman of Chatoyant Beagles add: "Raw feeding can be cheaper than dried food. While there are some ready-prepared and pre-packaged raw foods which may be quite costly we just do very basic raw food, i.e. meat and mixer, and this is definitely cheaper than dried and we feel better for our Beagles."

Food Allergies

Unfortunately, just like humans, Beagles sometimes react badly to certain foods. It is important to look out for signs, especially itchy skin, but also rubbing of the face on the floor or carpet, excessive scratching, ear infections, hot patches, and rash on the chin and face.

The most **common allergies** are to beef, dairy products, chicken, wheat, eggs, corn starch, and soy. As with any allergy, remove suspect items or try a special diet. Helpful **supplements** include quercetin, bromelain and papain, diffused eucalyptus oil, and local honey.

Beagles need diversity in their diets just like humans do, and if he has been eating the same food for months he may have grown sensitive to certain allergenic ingredients, typically grains and other carbohydrates. Even the protein might be at fault because this is often laced with antibiotics and hormones causing overreaction in the immune system.

Allergy testing offers a definitive diagnosis and pinpoints necessary environmental and dietary changes. The tests are expensive, costing $200+ / £120+.

Work with your vet to develop an allergy elimination diet to help identify the source of the issue. Then new foods are added back in one at a time to gauge your dog's reaction and response. They may also suggest natural supplements to help with detoxifying the immune system.

How Much to Feed?

There is no definite answer because it depends on a number of varying factors. **Your Beagle is unique.** Even with two the same age, they can have differing metabolic levels, with one being very energetic compared to the other, which might be a slouch!

The amount of daily exercise you are able to give your Beagle is a critical factor because they will burn off more calories the more they do and thus need to eat more without putting on weight.

As a general rule, smaller Beagles have faster metabolisms so require a higher amount of food per pound of body weight. Younger Beagles also need more food than seniors, who by that age have a slower metabolic rate.

The type of food you serve is also a factor. There are definitely some lesser quality (low priced) foods that may have the weight (bulk) but offer less in terms of nutrition and goodness.

Be slightly cynical when reading the recommended daily allowance on the labels because they are usually higher than need be. Remember this is from the manufacturer who profits the more your Beagle eats!

Treats

These are a great way to reward your Beagle for good behavior and also for training purposes, however there are some cautions to note. Many are **high in sugar** and can contain artificial additives, milk, and fat.

Good quality treats can have nutritional value, but you really don't want to overuse them; I suggest they make up a maximum of 15% of their total daily calorie intake. Try to use **praise as a reward** instead, so you are not always using treats every time he needs rewarding.

Don't forget that treats don't just come out of a packet or box, they can also include normal items such as steamed vegetables, apple slices, and carrot sticks.

A great way to reward and stimulate your Beagle is a toy that dispenses the treat (food) when he works a puzzle out. The best-known is perhaps the Kong. This chew toy is made of nearly indestructible rubber. Kong sells specially shaped treats and different things you can squeeze inside, but you can stuff it with whatever he likes best.

Nina Ottosson is a genius Swedish pioneer in the world of interactive dog puzzle toys. Her offerings come in a variety of levels of difficulty and in both plastic and wood.

TIP: Take a hot dog, cut it into 4ths along its length and then chop the long, skinny lengths into lots of little pieces. Cook in the microwave for at least 2 minutes longer than you would normally cook a hot dog. You will have 50+ pieces to use as rewards.

Some people like to fill toys with a treat such as peanut butter but be aware of "low sugar" or "no sugar" peanut butters. They often replace the sugar with the artificial sweetener Xylitol, which is toxic to dogs. Look for ones with no added sweeteners or salt. Ingredients should state 100% peanuts.

Ingredients — Be Careful!

Learning to understand the labels on the back of packaging is really important to understand the quality of food you are giving to your beloved Beagle.

Some manufacturers can use "cute" tricks to **disguise** the amount of grains in their product. They list them separately (to push them down the list order) but added together they can add up to a sizeable amount. The reverse is true, where they add all the meat ingredients together as one so it appears as the first listed ingredient — but check what else the food consists of!

Although milk contains several beneficial nutrients, it also contains a high proportion of the sugar lactose. As in humans, many dogs have **real difficulties digesting** lactose and as a result, milk products can bring on stomach pains, flatulence, diarrhea, and even vomiting.

When you see meat listed, this refers to the clean flesh of slaughtered animals (chicken, cattle, lamb, turkey, etc.). The flesh can include striated skeletal muscle, tongue, diaphragm, heart, esophagus, overlying fat and the skin, sinew, nerves, and blood vessels normally found with that flesh.

When you see meat by-products listed, this refers to the clean parts of slaughtered animals, not including meat. These include lungs, spleen, kidneys, brain, liver, blood, bone, some fatty tissue, and stomach and intestines freed of their contents (it doesn't include hair, horns, teeth, or hooves).

Don't mistake dry food as being very low in meat content compared to a wet food that lists fresh meat as an ingredient. Fresh meat consists of two-thirds water, so you need to discount the water when doing your comparisons between the two.

The **Guaranteed Analysis** on the label is very helpful, as it contains the exact percentages of crude protein, fat, fiber, and moisture.

Don't be scared off if the main ingredient is chicken meal rather than fresh beef. This is simply chicken that is dehydrated, and it contains more protein than fresh chicken, which is 80 percent water. The same is true for beef, fish, and lamb.

Look out for Sodium Tripolyphosphate (E451), an artificial preservative historically used as a component of detergents and other industrial products shown to cause vomiting.

Potassium Sorbate (E202) is a damaging skin, eye, and respiratory tract irritant shown to cause irreversible damage to blood cells, have a negative effect on immunity, and cancer-causing characteristics.

Iron Oxide (E172) is a known skin and eye irritant that causes lung inflammation.

Poultry Flavour is animal "digest" chemically treated with enzymes and/or acids to produce a flavor that may not have to contain any real meat.

Sharon Hardisty of Blunderhall Beagles recommends: "This excellent independent website grades all dog foods and gives them stars up to 5, and explains why. It shows that some of the popular names are just well-marketed and not the best ingredients! Also paying more for food can be cheaper in the long run, as they actually need less of it. The website also shows how much each food costs to feed per day and where to buy it." https://www.allaboutdogfood.co.uk/

Obesity — the Silent Killer

Obesity is on the increase and is probably the greatest health threat facing dogs today. There are various medical reasons for excessive weight gain, so if your Beagle fails to lose weight (despite your best efforts), then do get them checked out by your vet.

That said, obesity is mostly caused by us humans feeding too much and/or not exercising our dogs enough. Dogs are considered overweight when they're carrying 10–15% more than their ideal body weight and obese when carrying 20–25% over their ideal. Obesity is defined as an excess of body fat, to a degree where it impairs health, welfare, and quality of life.

Female dogs are more likely to become obese than male dogs, and neutered dogs are more prone to gaining weight. An overweight Beagle is likely to be experiencing constant pain, and an optimal diet could help them live longer.

Our own weight is our responsibility, but for the majority of pets, their weight is determined by you, their owner. Obesity alone can decrease dogs' life expectancy by 2.5 years. Fat (adipose tissue) is not only extra weight to carry, extra exertion, it secretes hormones affecting appetite, inflammation, insulin sensitivity, and bodily functions.

Here are some other medical issues caused or made worse by obesity: Respiratory problems, metabolic and endocrine disorders, cancers, skin disorders, orthopedic disease, kidney dysfunction, circulatory issues, diabetes, osteoarthritis, hypothyroidism, congestive heart failure, and intervertebral disc disease.

TIP: Reassess how much you feed your Beagle. Many owners stick to the same amount religiously, but things change over time. At an ideal body weight they should have a visible waist, both from the top and the side (tucked in and up), and you should be able to feel their ribs and spine, without excessive fat coverage.

Photo Credit: Sharon Hardisty of Blunderhall Beagles.

TIP: Don't rely solely on your vet to tell you if your Beagle is overweight. This conversation is an awkward one and many vets may find it easier to not say anything. Plus, they are busy dealing with the current medical issues in front of them so it may get missed.

Don't rely on your Beagle to stop eating when he is full! No, they will eat anything they see in front of them just because it's available!

Avoid genetically engineered, carb-loaded, and chemically laced foods. A high-fat, low-to-moderate protein, ultra-low-carb diet is best for your Beagle. Dogs (and cats) have NO requirement to intake starch (aka sugar). They can thrive with no carbohydrates in their diet, yet the average pet food ranges from 30 percent to 70 percent carbs!

Natural Medicines — Herbs for a Healthy Diet

Herbal medicine is the oldest recorded form of medicine, involving the use of plants or their extracts as medicine. Before they were used for medicine, plants were used as food for flavor and nutrition. Now most food comes in packaging, ready-made or processed with sugar and salt and other additives used for flavor.

Instead, why not try adding some herbs to your Beagle's diet? Parsley, basil, mint, oregano, sage, rosemary, and thyme are aromatic and flavor-filled because of their volatile oil components. Freshly chopped or dried, they can be added to meals every day, using anywhere from a pinch to a teaspoon, depending on your dog's size and health.

Spices and seeds often used in Eastern cooking such as turmeric, ginger, fennel seed, cayenne, and cinnamon all have health benefits. These are most commonly added to food as powders, although turmeric and ginger can be used fresh, and fennel seed is often made into a tea.

Feeding Older Beagles

Once your Beagle passes the age of 8, he can be considered a "senior," and his body has different requirements than those of a young dog — you may notice signs of your dog slowing down, putting on weight, or having joint issues. This is the time to discuss and involve your vet in considering switching to a senior diet.

Because his body's metabolism is slowing down, the adult diet he is on may have too many calories that **cannot be burned off** with the amount of exercise he is capable of. This isn't your fault, so don't feel guilty.

Don't let the pounds pile on. They are much harder to take off than put on, and his weight **literally affects his longevity**, as more strain is being put on his internal organs and joints. A senior diet is specially formulated to have a lower calorie count. They tend to be higher in fiber to prevent constipation, which senior dogs can be prone to.

Some breeders also suggest supplements such as glucosamine and chondroitin, which assist joints.

The opposite problem is loss of appetite. It may be as simple as needing a change of food, but it could be issues with his teeth. A moister food may help, but first get his teeth checked by your vet.

A breeder friend of mine told me of his aging dogs barking for no apparent reason. He started feeding them Pro Plan Bright Minds and saw a difference for the better within a few weeks. He says they are more alert and the barking for no apparent reason just stopped.

What the Breeders Advise on Feeding and Diet

Natasha Bell of Alfadais Beagles: "As a rule Beagles are generally very good eaters and will eat almost anything; it is, I feel, their one true love! Therefore I always like to feed them at least twice a day, morning and evening, varying their meals to include some favorites a few times a week such as cheese & fish. They do well on most foods whether it be dried kibble (I always use a grain free fish-based kibble such as Salmon & Potato), wet food, or a raw-based diet, guidelines for most foods are just that … guidelines, all dogs are different very much like us so it's important to use your own common sense and eye to assess whether your Beagle is doing well on a particular food and increase or decrease if necessary, taking into account the amount of exercise they receive and if their coat and eyes look healthy.

"Food can also be an ideal tool when used for training — the way to a Beagle's heart is food! With young puppies I tend to use kibble for this, as treats can be a little rich for those tiny tummies, moving on to treats when they are a little older.

"What you feed your Beagle can very much reflect in their behavior and health. You get out what you put in so it's important to do a little research and get this right, you will, as a result have a healthy happy little hound."

Stacey Burrows of Summerlily Beagles: "Beagles are prone to weight gain and will use their dark eyes, melting expression, and act like they have never been fed in the hope of getting a little more! I personally like Royal Canin Medium Junior to rear puppies on, as I find they do well on it, keeping them chunky and providing bone and substance which in turn gives them something to 'grow into.' My adults are fed on a locally produced complete food which is almost identical to Arden Grange. Neutered dogs are also prone to weight gain and benefit from a diet with less protein. I always recommend that looking from a bird's eye view that you should be able to see a waistline; if you can't, slightly reduce the quantity fed and if the waistline is too prominent, increase their food intake."

Edy Ballard of Ironwood Beagles: "Do not buy your Beagle a cheap food, being 'penny wise and pound foolish,' as the saying goes. Ask your breeder what brand of food your puppy was started on and for recommendations on good brands to feed. Also, don't feed young puppies grain-free formulas, as they need the extra carbohydrates for growth and energy. Look for high-quality brands where meat is the first ingredient. Ironwood puppies and dogs are fed Purina Pro-Plan Focus formulas."

Sam Goldberg of BeagleHealth.info: "I tend to rear puppies on Royal Canin, as this seems to suit my Beagles, but I feed the adults on a modified BARF diet. They get kibble such as Arden Grange with some raw food. I like to add things such as raw chicken wings, which they chew and help keep teeth clean. We have a local supplier, Durham Animal Feeds, which do have outlets around the U.K. and produce complete raw diets, as well as grain-free kibble. I also use dried empty cow hooves as general chews, which they pick up and chew from time to time."

TIP: Great natural treats — CARROTS. They serve to help keep their teeth clean and are much healthier for them than commercial biscuits, etc. Dogs LOVE them! Our grocery store sells 15-pound bags for $10. Economical, healthy treat!

TIP: For upset stomachs with puppies — keep a can of pure pumpkin on hand — not the pie mix, but pure pumpkin. Give a tablespoon on top of dry food, once a day. Alternate this with a tablespoon of plain yogurt the next day. This is great for stomach/digestive problems.

Managing Your Beagle's Activity

In addition to taking your Beagle for long walks — as much as an hour in duration every day — plan on incorporating hearty games of fetch, runs, and hikes into your dog's life. The more activity the better. These outings not only keep your dog's body in good shape, they stimulate his mind. Beagles like to think they're working.

Photo Credit: Hazel Deans of Gempeni Beagles.

As scent hounds, they have an innate instinct to track. Use that as part of the game. You can actually purchase bottled animal scents online and in feed stores. Soak toys with the scent and hide them for your dog to track. Your Beagle will love these kinds of games because it's what he was born to do!

Also, food is a powerful motivator for a real "chow hound" like a Beagle. Hiding and sniffing out treats provides one of these dogs with endless entertainment. It's all a treasure hunt as far as your pet is concerned.

The bottom line is there's rarely "too much" activity for a Beagle. Seize every opportunity to get your dog outdoors and doing something to avoid problem behaviors, separation anxiety, and destruction created by the simple fact that the poor dog is bored out of his mind.

Your Beagle likes routine, so establish one and stick to it as much as possible. Just because you have a garden or yard does not mean that you don't need to walk your dog. He needs mental stimulation as well as physical.

Note that when Beagles are young, exercise should be limited in as much as pounding pavements should be avoided. I think it is imperative not to over-exercise puppies under 6 months. I have seen baby puppies end up as adults with very unsound joints, as they have been taken for too many long walks. Young puppies have soft bones/joints like a child, and they don't really firm up until 5–6 months old. Over exercising can upset the growth plates that can cause weakness in the elbows, pasterns, and stifles.

Free running for short bursts of a few minutes at a time is fine, and as the puppy reaches around six months, the periods of free running can be increased.

Once muscles and bones are grown when the dog is around twelve months, really they can take as much exercise as the owner wants to give. This should be on a daily basis and not confined to weekends!

Beagles are intelligent and need mental stimulation in addition to physical training, and may become fractious if their lifestyle is too sedentary.

As a rule of thumb, around **half an hour free running daily** when they are adults will be enough to keep your Beagle toned, and this coupled with a good-sized garden to patrol will keep him on his toes.

Do consider summer temperatures — your Beagle has a fur coat they can't take off, and they don't have the same cooling-down options available to us. If you feel you are too hot or start to sweat, then don't walk your dog at that time of day. Always make sure that you have water available if you go out for a walk.

TIP: Think about hot sidewalks (pavements). Before a walk, place the back of your hand on the ground and hold it there. If you cannot hold it there for a minute, then it is too hot for your Beagle. Their paws are extremely sensitive and can get burned or even stick to tarmac or other hard surfaces in hot weather.

Ideas for cooling them down include: Having a paddling pool, hosing or sponging them down, or providing a fan near them (a wet towel placed in front of the fan adds a bit of moisture to the air as an added bonus).

Photo Credit: Stacey Burrows of Summerlily Beagles.

Sam Goldberg of BeagleHealth.info: "The general rule which I like is five to ten minutes per month of age in young puppies for exercise. So a pup which has just finished vaccinations would get 15–30 minutes vigorous exercise a day maximum. Remember as well that this includes playing chase games around the house with an older Beagle. Too much exercise and your Beagle puppy will end up with fine bone and leggy, as they only grow when asleep."

Collar or Harness?

Regardless of breed, I'm not a big fan of using a traditional collar. I wouldn't enjoy a choking sensation and assume my dog wouldn't either. That said, many breeders prefer collars. My current favorite on-body restraints are the harnesses that look like vests. They offer a point of attachment for the lead on the back between the shoulders.

This arrangement directs pressure away from the neck and allows for easy, free movement. Young dogs are less resistant to this system and don't strain against a harness the way they will with a collar.

It's best to take your Beagles with you to the pet store to get a proper fit. Sizing for a dog is much more unpredictable than you might think. I have seen dogs as large as 14 lbs. / 6.35 kg take an "Extra Small," depending on their build. Regardless of size, harnesses retail in a range of $20–$25 / £11.88–£14.85.

Standard Leash or Retractable?

The decision to buy a standard, fixed-length leash or a retractable lead is, for the most part, a matter of personal preference. Some facilities like groomers, vet clinics, and dog daycares ask that you not use a retractable lead on their premises. The long line represents a trip and fall hazard for other human clients.

Fixed-length leashes often sell for as little as $5 / £3, while retractable leads are less than $15 / £9.

Learning to respond to your control of the leash is an important behavioral lesson for your Beagle. Do not **drag a dog** on a lead or **jerk him**. If he sits down and refuses to budge, pick him up. Don't let the dog be in charge of the walk or you'll have the devil's own time regaining the upper hand.

Beagles love to get out in the world and "sniff the trail." They will associate the lead with adventures and time with you. Don't be at all surprised if your dog picks up words associated with excursions like go, out, car, drive, or walk and responds accordingly.

Never let a Beagle off the leash in an open, unfenced area! They run like the wind and don't come when they are called, especially when they are chasing down an interesting scent.

Dog Walking Tips

Active dogs like Beagles are "into" the whole walking experience. This is an excellent opportunity to use the activity to build and reinforce good behaviors on command.

Teach your Beagle to sit by using the word and making a downward pointing motion with your finger or indicating the desired direction with the palm of your hand. Do not attach the lead until your dog complies, rewarding his patience with the words he most wants to hear: "Okay, let's go!"

If your dog jerks or pulls on the leash, stop, pick up the dog, and start the walk over with the "sit" command. Make it clear that the walk ceases when the dog misbehaves. Praise your dog for walking well on the end of the lead and for stopping when you stop. Reinforce positive behaviors during walks. Your dog will get the message and show the same traits during other activities.

Veronica and Rosie Longman of Chatoyant Beagles: "The trainers we work with recommend stopping if the puppy pulls, only walking on again when the puppy has returned to you. Or turning and walking the other way. Puppies quickly learn pulling means no walking and will walk quietly at your side."

Sam Goldberg of BeagleHealth.info: "If you have a foody puppy try using a small treat in your hand to get a puppy to walk forward on a lead if you have a very reluctant one."

Beagles and Agility in the U.K.

Susie Arden of Madika Beagles gives us an overview of her experiences of participating in agility in the United Kingdom.

"Agility shows mostly comprise of Collie and Spaniel types, but you can find the odd Beagle who excels at agility too. To start with you do need a good relationship with your Beagle and obviously a good amount of obedience for such a fast sport. "Not many owners show their

Photo Credit: Susie Arden of Madika Beagles.

Beagles as well as compete at agility, but I successfully do both and my Beagle Emma — Barterhound Rosebud At Madika JW ShCM AW(S) — proved it can be done when she became the first Beagle to gain her Junior Warrant and Agility Warrant, as well as her Show Certificate of Merit.

"To claim an Agility Warrant, the dog gains points (only from K.C. Shows) for clear rounds (1 point for Jumping class and 2 points for agility class) with more points gained for wins and places. The Bronze requires 200 points, the Silver 400 points, and 800 for Gold.

"It all began when I entered Emma in an agility competition at a fun dog show. Despite never having done any agility before, she won 1st prize; this inspired me to take her to agility training class, vital for any thoughts of competing. Training takes time and patience, especially to master the 'weaves,' but the reward is immense, especially when it all comes together in the ring.

Photo Credit: Susie Arden of Madika Beagles.

"Kennel Club shows are Graded. A new dog and handler start at Grade 1 and have to 'win out' of the grades, the highest grade being 7. Only grade 7 dogs are allowed to compete in Championship classes where CCs are on offer.

"At just over 4 years old, Emma 'won out' at her first K.C. show and retired from regular classes as a Grade 7 after having her eye removed at 8 years old, though at nearly 10 years old she still enjoys training and competing in the fun classes.

"Dottie — Madika Spot On JW AW(B) — is Emma's daughter who in just her first 8 months competing gained her Agility Warrant Bronze and won her way into Grade 6. Dottie is just a youngster at not yet 3 years old and is still learning, but already she is the only Beagle to have won a Reserve C.C. in the show ring, as well as an Agility Warrant.

"There's never a dull moment with a Beagle and agility is no different. They are fun to train and to compete with, as you just never know what they'll do, which always proves quite a crowd pleaser.

"There are owners of Beagles who struggle with their 'nose to the ground,' but fortunately this is something I've never had to deal with, though Dottie usually manages to do 'something' unexpected. At her first show, she left the ring to investigate a couple sitting with a flask of tea, and on another occasion she left the ring to say hello to another dog, though on both occasions quickly came running back and carried on. This fun-loving girl has also tried to pick up the numbers and run off with them!!

"Agility is fun and very rewarding. It also keeps your Beagle fit and active and does help making it a more contented pet; the winning is just a bonus.

Claudia Anderson of TwainHeart Beagles: "Scent Work, a relatively new AKC event, is a natural fit for Beagles. It exercises the Beagle's in-bred instincts and encourages owners to develop a keener attention to their Beagle's behavior. The sport mimics the work of detection dogs that find everything from agricultural contraband to drugs to people.

"In AKC Scent Work trials, dogs find specific odors (birch, anise, clove, cypress) in various kinds of environments.

"While Scent Work is a new offering for AKC, other organizations have offered trials in scent detection for several years, including the National

Association of Canine NoseWork (NACSW), the United Kennel Club, and Sniffing Dog Sports. There are several trainers throughout the U.S. that offer classes in scent detection."

Play Time and Tricks

Beagles are smart, so give your dog plenty of toys, and observe what he does and doesn't like to do. You'll know soon enough if he's willing to learn tricks with you.

Photo Credit: Janet Kautz/Claudia Anderson of TwainHeart Beagles.

In obedience training, your Beagle will learn a basic set of commands like sit, stay, and heel. These commands can be used as the basis to get your dog to respond to cues to perform tricks, but only if he is agreeable. There's no guarantee your Beagle will cooperate. He may just walk away. It doesn't hurt to try, but never try to force your pet to do something he really doesn't want to do.

Always offer praise and show pleasure for correct responses. This makes training just another form of play — and **Beagles love to play!**

The speed with which your dog will amass and destroy a collection of toys may shock you. Avoid soft rubber toys — they shred into small pieces, which the dog will swallow. Opt for rope toys instead or chew toys that can withstand the abuse. You can buy items made out of this tough material in the $1–$5 / £0.59–£2.97 range. Don't buy anything with a squeaker or any other part that presents a choking hazard.

Never give your dog rawhide or pig's ears, which soften and present a choking hazard. Also avoid cow hooves, which can splinter and puncture the cheek or palate.

Sam Goldberg of BeagleHealth.info: "I agree regarding the rawhide and pig's ears, but I do use cow's hooves. They soften well in the rain and the Beagles love them. So far I have never seen them splinter. I do like the antlers, but the dental vets hate them, as they believe they cause teeth fractures.

"The cheap tunnels for children make good skills toys for puppies, as do Kong toys with dangling ends. For a new puppy in his first home, stuffing a Kong with food and freezing it makes a good toy to keep a puppy occupied whilst teaching being left for periods alone."

Play time is important, especially for a dog's natural desire to chase. Try channeling this instinct with toys and games. If a dog has no stimulation and has nothing to chase, they can start to chase their own tail, which can lead to problems. Dogs that don't get enough exercise are also more likely to develop problem behaviors like chewing, digging, and barking.

Toys can be used to simulate the dog's natural desire to hunt. For example, when they catch a toy, they will often shake it and bury their teeth into it, simulating the killing of their prey.

Allow your dog to fulfill **a natural desire** to chew. This comes from historically catching their prey and then chewing the carcass. Providing chews or bones can prevent your dog from destroying your home. Deer antlers are wonderful toys for a Beagle; most love them. They do not smell, are all-natural, and do not stain or splinter. I recommend the antlers that are not split: they last longer.

Playing with your dog is not only a great way of getting them to use up their energy, but it is also a **great way of bonding** with them as they have fun. Dogs love to chase and catch balls, but make sure that the ball is too large to be swallowed.

I also recommend having a toy mobile over the pen with various soft and hard toys hanging down, and I have a game that you hide food under and they have to move the pieces to get the food — great to make them use their senses. Puppies need to experience a variety of different textures, whether rubber, plastic, or soft fabrics.

Chapter 8 — Interested in Showing Your Beagle?

If you have purchased a show-quality Beagle and are planning to enter the world of dog shows and the dog fancy, you have a whole education in front of you. If you have not already done so, you will want to begin to attend dog shows and to make connections in the world of the dog fancy to acquire the training to participate with your Beagle, or to hire someone to show the animal for you.

Photo Credit: Carol Herr of Roirdan Beagles at Westminster. Carol comments: "Yes, my little Beagle won the best of 13" variety at Westminster. It was definitely a great surprise, especially under a very well-known and respected judge, Doug Johnson."

Sam Goldberg of Molesend Beagles: "Firstly talk to the breeder (who is hopefully a person who is serious about Beagles). An experienced breeder will be happy to mentor you or suggest someone in your area who can give tips and advice. Finding a local ringcraft class for show people will help with socializing with different breeds and also tips for showing."

Veronica and Rosie Longman of Chatoyant Beagles: "If you might be interested in showing, always tell the breeder before purchasing a puppy, and they will then ensure you get a show-quality puppy (as far as one can tell at 8 weeks). Be sure to buy from a kennel that does actually show on a regular basis also."

The best thing you can do if you are planning to show your puppy is socializing them once they have settled in their new home. The work you put in at this stage of your puppy's life will shape them for life, so you need to get it right, take it slowly, and build it up gently. Remember: They are only babies, and they need to know you are there for them and are in charge of every situation.

Photo Credit: Patricia Eschbach of Spring Creek Beagles.

Your puppy needs to be happy for a judge to run their hands all over them, so it is very important to get them used to this.

When your Beagle puppy is happy for you to be able to touch them all over, you can get your trusted friends to do the same. Start at the head, look in their ears and eyes, and run your hands all down their back and down their legs.

What Dogs Are Qualified to Participate?

For a dog to participate in a dog show, it must be registered with the governing body for that exhibition. For instance, dogs registered with the American Kennel Club that are 6 months or older on the day of the show are eligible to enter AKC sponsored events. Spayed or neutered dogs are not eligible, nor are dogs with disqualifying faults according to the accepted standard for the breed.

It's generally easier to show a male, as opposed to a female, because females can be hard on their coat and change behavior during their heat cycles.

Joining a Breed Club

When you attend a dog show, find out about joining a breed-specific club in your area. Such groups usually sponsor classes to teach the basics in handling and showing the breed or will have contacts to put you in touch with individual teachers.

Breed club membership is also important to learn the culture of the dog fancy and to meet people in the show world. You will begin by participating in smaller, local shows to learn the ropes before entering an event that will garner points toward sanctioned titles within a governing group's system.

Photo Credit: Edy Ballard of Ironwood Beagles.

There are also "fun matches" that a new dog owner can participate in open to dogs from 3–6 months of age. Here they can get an idea of how dog show judging takes place. It's also a great training ground for that future show prospect.

The more you know about your breed, its care and maintenance, and the handling of them, the better you will be in the show ring. Study your country's parent kennel club's official breed standard.

Hiring a Professional

It is not uncommon for people who own show quality animals to hire professional handlers to work with the dogs. If you are interested in going this route, be sure to interview several handlers and to get a full schedule of their rates. Attend a show where they are working with a

dog and watch them in action. Ask for references, and contact the people whose names you are given.

Entrusting a handler with the care of your dog is an enormous leap of faith. You want to be certain you have hired someone with whom you are completely comfortable and with whom your Beagle has an observable rapport.

Photo Credit: Joan Wurst of Everwind Beagles.

Don't Be Put Off by Fear

My advice to folks who are interested in starting to show is go to several shows and watch the dogs in the ring. Talk to the folks at the sidelines; most are very happy to talk dogs with you.

Find a successful show person to evaluate the dog you plan to start showing. Although anybody can show a dog, you need to get an objective appraisal of your dog's qualities. To qualify as a show dog, it can't have any disqualifying faults, so it is important you find a mentor who can honestly help you evaluate your dog.

I also advise you to attend conformation classes in your area if possible, and be sure your dog is well-socialized. Most local Kennel Clubs offer these classes at very reasonable rates. Presentation and the dog's attitude are also a very important factor. Shy and timid dogs usually don't do well at a dog show.

Don't forget that judges' assignments are to assess the breeding stock quality of the exhibits before them via the official breed standard description, observations on movement, and their hands-on experience. There are good judges and the opposite. Many owners have found that performance events, such as obedience, agility, rally, and therapy dog provide great satisfaction in lieu of conformation events.

Of course, you always hope your dog will win. If you have done all your homework, and your dog is a good representative of the breed, you should walk in the ring with confidence and present your dog as best as possible. There is no such thing as a perfect dog, and a good handler will know how to hide the faults and show off the best traits.

I always found going to a dog show exciting. You should always think of it as fun. It will give you an opportunity to meet many people who are also fanciers of your particular breed.

Although it is a competition, whether you win or lose, you should always be a good sport. Remember, there is always another show and another judge and different competition. After a while, you will get to know which judges like a particular type or style of your breed.

Show Tips and Advice

Stacking is how the dog stands naturally and when placed in position. This helps the judges see all areas of the dog's structure to evaluate against the breed standard and to allow the judges to feel the dogs bone structure and muscles.

Hazel Deans of Gempeni Beagles on how to train your puppy to stack:

"Stand your puppy on a non-slip surface on a table. Front legs should be straight and parallel as should the hocks. The aim is to hold the puppy's head under the chin and hold the tail straight up. Take care your puppy doesn't jump or fall off the table, as they can move very fast! You may find your puppy won't cooperate and refuses to be stacked. This is normal! Be confident, firm and tell him to stand.

"Reward the puppy with praise and treat only if he stacks. If he refuses, keep calm and put him on the floor without praise and try again later. The puppy will be less likely to stack if he is lively and energetic. Make it easier by waiting until he has tired a little.

Photo Credit: Hazel Deans of Gempeni Beagles

"He will soon learn what you want him to do. Start with very short periods, just a few seconds of stacking gradually increasing the time. It may seem as if he will never stack for you, but don't worry, one day he will suddenly do it! Once standing well on the table start also standing him on the ground."

Make sure you are well-organized. Get to the show at least an hour before you are in the ring, as this will give you and your dog time to settle down.

Make sure you have your ring number on when you enter the ring. Make a strong entrance — you only get one chance to make an impression. Remember, the judge will look across the ring from time to time, so have your dog facing the judge even when you are relaxed. Always keep an eye on the judge.

Before you set off, have your arm in an L shape. It will help you keep in a straight line and have more control. Look at something in front of you, keep your eyes on it, and move towards it. Say your dog's name, then say move.

Never give treats when you are moving your dog, as your dog will look up at you, and you need them to go in a straight line. In addition, don't give treats when the judge is going over your dog. Save the treat your dog loves the most for shows, not training, so you can get their attention even more so.

Don't get boxed in a corner at the show; give yourself plenty of room by not standing too close to other exhibiters.

Always dress smart, wear good shoes you can run in, and if you're a woman, wear a sports bra.

Hold your head up, try to look confident, and look like a winner. The judge needs to know you can hold your own and show your dog off in the big ring. If you look too shy, they may think you are not up to the job of representing your breed in the group ring.

Always have a cloth to wipe your dog's mouth dry. Do this just before it's your turn to stand your dog for the judge. It makes showing the bite so much easier.

Warm your dog up before you go in the ring by having a little practice run.

Finally, always take your dog to show in good, clean condition.

Edy Ballard of Ironwood Beagles: "My best advice is to get a mentor. The breeder from whom you buy your show puppy is a good place to start. Dog showing can be a very fun sport, but it helps in the beginning to have someone along to teach you the finer points of the show ring, from show grooming to finding your ring times. Remember that it is also very competitive, and like all competitive endeavors, you'll find a wide range of personalities participating. Try to get to know the people who have a positive attitude and display good sportsmanship. Remember to always have fun with your dog, after all, he's your family's 'best in show' and he's doing his best to please you."

The Westminster Dog Show and Crufts

So how does an owner get to take part in the famous Westminster Dog Show in the United States?

It is a requirement that in order to compete, your dog must already have earned a major toward their AKC championship or have an AKC championship. The entry forms are sent out in October of the previous year, and there is a limit to the number of entries that are accepted. This number has increased the last few years, and most entries are now accepted if submitted properly within a few days of the first acceptance date in December.

You can submit entries online, via USPS, or through a third-party entry service. In the past, it was more difficult to get your entry received before the limit was reached. Since the class judging moved from Madison Square Garden to the Piers it has become much easier, as the limit is higher.

Dog shows are the second oldest sport, next to the Kentucky Derby. It is a great sport, where you can meet some wonderful friends, including from other countries. It can be a family affair, where children can start to compete against each other in the junior classes as early as 8 years old.

There is a significant difference between showing at an AKC show and showing at a Kennel Club show. Most AKC shows occur over just ONE day, Westminster being one of the exceptions, and the vast majority of shows are between 500–1000 dogs total. There are frequently multiple shows in consecutive days in the same venue, and the chance to win points at each event. If you are just getting started showing in the U.S., visit a show without entering. Many AKC shows have "Dog Show Tours" or will pair you with an experienced person if you are looking to get started. You can find information on their website.

The world-famous Crufts show in the U.K. is the only show in the U.K. where dogs have to qualify to enter by winning at least a 3rd place in their breed at another championship show in the preceding year.

Despite being another show, Crufts has its own personality unlike any other event. The anticipation and the razzmatazz make it extra special.

There are plenty of shows apart from Crufts. If you think you might like to exhibit your Beagle, there are different levels of shows that you can go to. A good place to start would be with a "companion show" — dogs don't have to be registered with the Kennel Club, and entries are taken on the day. Often in addition to some classes for pedigree dogs, there will be classes for such things as "best condition," "prettiest face," and such like. These are just for fun, but they can be a good place for a novice to practice.

Following this the next step is a "limit show." Here entries are made in advance and it is confined to dogs who have not won major awards.

The "open show" is the next level and here any dogs can enter, including champions. Breeds will be scheduled and points can be achieved towards a Junior Warrant.

Photo Credit: Carol and Lori Norman of Lokavi Beagles.

The highest level is the "championship show." This is where a Cruft's qualification can be won, as well as the all-important Challenge Certificate. To be a champion, a dog needs to win three challenge certificates under three separate judges in order to achieve their title. All the males in the breed compete in their classes, and then all the winners compete against each other to win the dog CC. The same thing happens with all the bitches and then the bitch CC is awarded. The best dog and the best bitch compete against each other to produce the "best of breed."

More information can be found on the Kennel Club website, including addresses of local clubs who can help in training for shows: http://www.thekennelclub.org.uk/.

Chapter 9 — Grooming

Beagles shed moderately for most of the year, but their coats are short and tight. Weekly brushing will help to cut down on the amount of cast-off hair around the house.

As **soon as your Beagle is home**, work on desensitizing him to your touch. This will help when you come to groom him and also when you have to visit the vet's. Start slowly to begin with and build up the time as he seems comfortable. Touch areas such as his gums and nails so these areas can be maintained by you.

Don't allow yourself to get caught in the "my Beagle doesn't like it" trap, which is an excuse many owners will use to avoid regular grooming sessions. When your Beagle dictates whether they will permit a grooming session, you are setting a dangerous precedent. In time, your Beagle **will love** to be tickled, rubbed, and scratched in certain favorite places. Grooming is a great source of pleasure and a way to bond together.

Regular brushing helps your Beagle in many ways. Aerating the coat ensures healthy growth by promoting good blood circulation. It helps to keep grease levels down which can block pores and cause sebaceous cysts. He will also **shed less hair** around your house.

If you don't brush (groom) them, their loose hairs become matted, forming heavy wads, which can cause skin complaints and soreness.

Also, toenails need to be checked every 4 weeks; be sure they are not hitting the floor. One can gauge this by listening to the dog walk. You should not hear the nails touching the floor; they should be "just off" the floor. This is important, as it can change the gait of the dog and eventually cause knee or hip problems.

Every week, the owner needs to trim hairs around the eyes so the corneas do not get scratched. Very importantly, clean around the eyes once a day to clean up excessive tearing and prevent tear staining.

In terms of brushes, the standard options include:

- **Bristle** brushes, which work well with all coats from long to short. They remove dirt and debris and distribute natural oils throughout the coat.

- **Wire-pin** brushes, which are for medium to long coats and look like a series of pins stuck in a raised base.

- **Slicker** brushes are excellent for smoothing and detangling longer hair.

You can often find combination, two-headed brushes. They'll save you a little money and make your grooming sessions easier.

Each of these types of brush costs less than $15 / £9 and often less than $10 / £6.

Stacey Burrows of Summerlily Beagles: "I think a ballpoint slicker brush should be used as the metal teeth on a normal slicker brush can be quite sharp."

Personally, I find the best grooming tool to use on your Beagle at home is a wire pin brush — brush your Beagle from head to toe, moving in the direction of hair growth. If you come across a matt or tangle, try to work through it with a wide-tooth comb. If you absolutely cannot get it out, you can cut it out. To do so, pinch the hair below the matt as close to your Beagle's skin as you can — this will help to make sure you do not accidentally cut your dog's skin — then just cut the matt free.

Spraying the coat with a conditioner before combing will keep it shining and clean.

TIP: A friend of mine swears by the **Tangle Teezer** brush. Although it's for women's hair, it apparently works like a charm. She says brushing is now fun and relaxing because her dog believes he is getting a massage.

Grooming/brushing sessions are an excellent opportunity to examine your dog's skin to do a **quick health check**. Look for any growths, lumps, bumps, or wounds. Also have a good look at his ears, eyes, and mouth. Check between paw pads for any balls of matted fur, which can become hard with dirt and grease, causing pain.

While you can learn how to trim your Beagle's coat yourself, it can be a challenging task that might be best left to the professionals. A professional groomer will know how to handle your Beagle's thick coat and will be able to trim it according to your preferences.

Eyes

Your Beagle's eyes should be clear and bright, with no excessive discharge apart from that left over from sleeping.

Older dog's eyes may show signs of becoming cloudy; this could be a sign of cataracts, and if you are worried, then it is worth speaking to your vet.

You should wipe their eyes regularly with a warm, damp cloth to remove the buildup of secretions in the corners of the eyes. This can be both unattractive and uncomfortable for the dog, as the hair becomes glued together. If this build up is not removed every day, it can quickly become a cause of **bacterial yeast growth** that can lead to smelly eye infections.

Cleaning the Ears

Those lovely, floppy ears (pinna) help waft scent up as they hunt and stop things such as seeds getting inside them, but they don't let much air get into your Beagle's ear canals, creating a ripe environment for fungal and bacterial infections. Your Beagle's ears should be frequently checked. Look for a dark discharge or regular scratching, as this can signal an infection. Affected ears have a stronger smell than usual.

When grass seeds get into the ear canal they can be extremely painful & distressing for your dog. Left in they can rupture the ear drum and move into the inner ear causing serious disease. They have even been known to track all the way up legs to burst out of elbows!

Look out for warning signs: sudden onset of head shaking or rubbing, holding the head at a tilt with the affected ear down, distress and/or whimpering, lameness, cysts or swellings or discharge from between the toes, or swellings around the feet.

Avoiding letting your Beagle run through or roll in long grasses, keep the hair around the ears and feet **trimmed reasonably short** so the seeds have less to attach to, and check him over after walks.

Beagles that have a lot of hair growing inside the ear can struggle with infection, as the hair can prevent normal healthy wax leaving the ear area. Trim the hair inside the ears with safety scissors (blunted end).

Ear mites can become a problem if your dog comes into contact with an infected animal. Too small to be seen by the naked eye, a bad ear mite infestation can cause the dog a lot of unrest and distress through itchiness. Both infections and ear mites can be diagnosed and treated easily with drops, antibiotics, or both, as prescribed by your vet.

There are many ear cleaning creams, drops, oils, rinses, solutions, and wipes formulated for cleaning ears that you can buy from your local pet store or veterinarians. You may prefer to use a home remedy that will just as efficiently clean your Beagle's ears, such as **Witch Hazel** or a 50:50 mixture of hydrogen peroxide and purified water.

On a weekly basis, use a cleaner to protect your dog's ears against these potential problems. Avoid a buildup of wax, which can lead to irritation and infection, as the normal bacteria and yeasts on the skin start to multiply. Look for signs of redness down the ear or Beagles displaying pain by shaking their head. Squirt the cleaner in the ear and then fold the flap over, massaging the cleaner into the base of the ear. Allow the dog to shake its head, and then clean the visible parts of the ear only with a cotton ball. Repeat on the other side. Most ear infections are not contagious from one dog to another; you just need to take care to continue treatment as advised even if the ear looks healed.

Ear powders, which can be purchased at any pet store, are designed to help keep your Beagle's ears dry while at the same time inhibiting the growth of bacteria that can lead to infections. You may want to apply a little ear powder after washing the inside of your dog's ears to help ensure that they are totally dry.

Bathing

A Beagle's minimal grooming needs beyond weekly brushing is a definite plus for this breed. The cleaner the dog's environment, the less odor will be present. Using a bed stuffed with cedar or other aromatic shavings can also be a huge help, but do be cautious about allowing your dog to come into contact with anything that might trigger an allergic reaction.

Bathing a Beagle too often will strip the skin of the necessary essential oils and leave the poor animal dried out and itchy. Usually Beagles only require a bath when they've gotten into something. When you do decide your pet really must have a bath, use tepid water and a good quality canine shampoo.

Veronica and Rosie Longman of Chatoyant Beagles: "Beagles do not smell, or if they do, it is a lovely smell. They only smell 'doggy' when wet — one of their great attractions."

If you do need to bathe your Beagle, give him a good brushing before you do. Fill your bathtub with a few inches of warm water then place your Beagle in it.

Beagles have low-hanging ears, which puts them at an increased risk for ear infections. Because the ears hang down over the head, there is not a lot of air circulation under the ear — if the area gets wet it could become a breeding ground for bacteria. To prevent **your Beagle's head getting wet,** clean his head and face with a warm, wet washcloth only. Rinse your dog's coat with a mixture of 1 tbs shampoo and 2 cups water, then pour over dog. Use clean, fresh water to remove all residue. Towel your pet dry and make sure he doesn't get chilled. The rinse is really the most important step of the whole procedure. If any shampoo is left in the coat, it will irritate the skin and lead to "hot spots."

TIP: Try using Chamois cloths to dry your Beagle. They work well, and they don't have to be laundered as much. They just air dry and can be washed in the washing machine. However, DO NOT put the Chamois in the dryer. I have found that they work much better than towels.

DON'T make the mistake of using human shampoo or conditioner on your Beagle, because they have a different pH balance than us and it will be too harshly acidic for their coat and skin, which can create skin problems. Purchase a shampoo that is **specially formulated** to be gentle and moisturizing on your Beagle's coat and skin, will not strip the natural oils, and will nourish your dog's coat to give it a healthy shine.

Nail Trimming

Coat maintenance is not the only grooming chore necessary to keep your Beagle in good shape. Even dogs that walk on asphalt or other rough surfaces will need to have their nails trimmed from time to time, although if you do walk your Beagle a lot they won't need as much trimming. If nails get too long, they can split and get damaged more easily. Check your Beagle once a month.

If your pet is agreeable, this is a job you can perform at home with a guillotine-style nail clipper especially designed for use with dogs. I prefer those with plier grips. They're easier to handle and quite cost effective, selling for under $20 / £11.88.

A Dremel sanding tool can be a good alternative to clippers for trimming your dog's nails. Never use a regular Dremel tool, as it will be too high speed and will burn your dog's toenails. Only use a slow-speed Dremel, such as Model 7300-PT Pet Nail Grooming Tool (approx. $40 / £20). You can also purchase the flexible hose attachment for the Dremel, which is much easier to handle and can be held like a pencil.

Snip off the nail tips at a 45-degree angle at the point where the nail begins to curve at the tip, before the point where the pink area, referred to as the quick, is visible.

Be careful not to cut too far down, otherwise you will hurt your Beagle and cause heavy bleeding. If this happens, don't panic. Use a piece of cotton or tissue and hold pressure on it until it stops bleeding. Buy some **styptic powder** just in case. This antiseptic clotting agent causes the vessels to contract, thereby stemming the blood loss. Apply to the nail only, and a warning — initially it will sting your Beagle.

Photo Credit: Carol Herr of Roirdan Beagles.

If you are apprehensive about performing this chore, ask your vet tech or groomer to walk you through it the first time.

Anal Glands

All dogs can suffer from blocked anal glands. Many dogs express them every time they poop (the sacs/glands are around a dog's anus, but occasionally the sacs fill with fluid and your Beagle will need some help to release the fluid).

He may scoot or rub his bottom on the ground or carpet (you may also notice a foul odor). If this occurs, the glands will need expressing to prevent an abscess from forming. This is a sensitive task and one that a veterinarian or an experienced groomer should perform.

If your dog is fed a healthy diet this should not be a problem. My vet suggested adding a probiotic to my dog's diet after she had a problem with her anal glands at about 9 years of age, and she has not had a problem since.

Fleas and Ticks

I'm including fleas and ticks under grooming because that's when they're usually found. Don't think that if your Beagle has "passengers" you're doing something wrong, or that the dog is at fault. This is a part of dog ownership. Sooner or later, it will happen. Address the problem, but don't panic.

To get rid of fleas, bathe your dog in warm water with a standard canine shampoo. I recommend you comb him at least once daily, every day during pest season with a flea comb that is fine-toothed to trap the live parasites. Submerge the comb in hot soapy water to kill the fleas. Do this on a white towel so you actually can see what's coming off your dog as you comb.

Wash the dog's bedding and any soft materials with which he has come in contact. Look for any accumulations of flea dirt, which is blood excreted by adult fleas. Wash the bedding and other surfaces daily for at least a week to kill any remaining eggs before they hatch.

While nobody likes to use chemicals on their dogs, it seems almost impossible to use anything else in the battle with fleas, ticks, and bugs! For the last decade or so, I have used a safe lawn product in my dog yards that kill fleas, ticks, spiders, mosquitoes, and more. I go by the directions and don't allow the dogs to go to those yards until after a rain or watering after application, since then I usually do not need to use any other products on the dogs. I do a lawn application at the end of March, the end of June, and the last one in September.

Do NOT use a commercial flea product on a puppy of less than 12 weeks of age, and be extremely careful with adult dogs. Most of the major products contain pyrethrum. The chemical can cause long-term neurological damage and even fatalities in small dogs.

TIP: Nexgard is a treatment for fleas and it also treats for heartworms, so it is time efficient. Also, Dawn dish soap kills fleas and is safe for all ages.

TIP: A collar, like the Seresto collar, is an innovative flea and tick collar that protects for up to 8 months by a slow release of insecticide — without the need to remember monthly applications.

If your Beagle is outside a lot, check for ticks on a regular basis, as these eight-legged parasites can carry diseases. Look out for warning signs such as lack of movement, swollen joints, fever, and loss of appetite.

If you find a tick, coat it with a thick layer of petroleum jelly for 5 minutes to suffocate the parasite and cause its jaws to release. Pluck the tick off with a pair of tweezers using a straight motion. An alternative is a tick remover, which is a tool similar to a bottle opener. Never just jerk a tick off a dog. The parasite's head stays behind and continues to burrow into the skin, making a painful sore.

Clean the wound with antiseptic and make sure to clean your tweezers with isopropyl alcohol to sterilize them. Keep an eye on the area where the tick was to see if an infection surfaces. If the skin remains irritated or infected, make an appointment with your veterinarian.

Many breeders are choosing to avoid harsh chemicals and over-vaccination, choosing instead to use homeopathic nosodes, natural wormers, and work on keeping their immune systems healthy. They tend to feed a raw, species-appropriate diet and don't treat their dogs for fleas unless they see them.

They also do regular worm counts on their older dogs to see if they actually have worms. **Diotomaceous Earth** added to the food daily helps to keep your dog clear of worms but if purchasing, make sure it's food grade. For dogs that don't like extras added to their food, I use **Four Seasons**. Ground pumpkin seeds can also be used.

Andrew and Tanya Gittins of Boomerloo Beagles have this advice: "We only treat for fleas if and when our dogs get them, as we don't like putting lots of chemicals onto them unnecessarily."

TIP: For a natural organic spray that repels ticks and fleas, try Herbal Defense Spray by PetzLife. Ruff on Bugs is a similar spray consisting of essential oils such as lemongrass, cinnamon, cedar, citronella, geranium, and rosemary, in non-GMO oils.

Home Dental Care

There are many products available to help with home dental care for your Beagle. Some owners opt for water additives that break up tartar and plaque, but in some cases dogs experience stomach upset. Dental sprays and wipes are also an option, but so is gentle gum massage to help break up plaque and tartar.

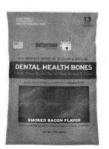

Most owners incorporate some type of dental chew in their standard care practices. Greenies Dental Chews for Dogs are popular and well tolerated in a digestive sense. An added plus is that dogs usually love them. The treats come in different sizes and are priced in a range of $7 / £4.21 for 22 "Teeny Greenies" and $25 / £15 for 17 "Large Greenies."

Indigenous Dental Health Bones are safe and highly digestible for all dog breeds and sizes. They are made with ascophyllum nodosum, a natural kelp harvested from the clean, cold North Atlantic seas of Canada, Iceland, and Norway. This kelp is a rich source of nutrients and is free from artificial colors and preservatives.

Your Beagle should have forty-two permanent teeth. At the front are six incisors in each jaw, which cut food. Next are the canines (two in each jaw), and these tear and hold food. Then the premolars (eight in each jaw) for cutting and tearing. At the very back of the mouth are the molars used for grinding — four on the top and six on the bottom.

The Beagle should have a scissor bite, meaning that the teeth in the top jaw should tightly overlap the bottom teeth. This is designed for gripping prey and allowing the Beagle to fulfil its natural role as a hunting hound.

Brushing your pet's teeth is the ultimate defense for oral health. This involves the use of both a canine-specific toothbrush and toothpaste. Never use human toothpaste, which contains fluoride toxic to your dog. Some dog toothbrushes resemble smaller versions of our own, but I like the models that just fit over your fingertip. I think they offer greater control and stability.

The real trick to brushing your pet's teeth is getting the dog comfortable with having your hands in his mouth. Start by just massaging the dog's face, and then progressing to the gums before using the toothbrush. In the beginning, you can even just smear the toothpaste on the teeth with your fingertip.

Schedule these brushing sessions for when the dog is a little tired, perhaps after a long walk. Don't apply pressure, which can stress him. Just move in small circular motions and stop when the Beagle has had enough of the whole business. If you don't feel you've done enough, stop. A second session is better than forcing your dog to do something he doesn't like and creating a negative association in his mind.

Even if you do practice a full home dental care routine, don't scrimp on annual oral exams in the vet's office. Exams not only help to keep the teeth and gums healthy, but also to check for the presence of possible cancerous growths.

TIP: If your dog will not let you brush their teeth, allow them to chew on knuckle bones, bull pizzles, cow ears, or trachea. These all help remove tartar and stimulate the gums.

TIP: "Dog breath" is best tackled with chewing on a raw meaty bone. If that doesn't suit, try raw fibrous vegetables (whole carrots, cabbage cores, broccoli stalks, etc.) or dried fish skin.

Chapter 10 — Training and Problem Behaviors

It is to your advantage to go through a basic obedience class with your dog. Beagles are intelligent, but stubborn dogs. All dogs respond well to a consistent routine and to a command "language." Provide both of these vital foundations to have a well-behaved pet.

Experts agree that most dogs can pick up between 165 and 200 words, but they can't extrapolate more than one meaning. If, for instance, your dog barks, you need to use the same command in response, like "quiet." If he picks something up, you might say "drop it."

For problem jumping, most owners go with "off" or "down." The point is to pick a set of words and use them over and over to create a basic vocabulary for your dog. Both the word and your tone of voice should convey your authority and elicit the desired response.

Beagles have a tremendous amount of energy that can be negatively expressed when they are bored or suffering from anxiety. Aggression toward other dogs is usually triggered by the Beagle's territorial urge to protect his "possessions" — his crate, his food bowl, his house, and you.

Understanding their working dog mentality is key to living successfully with this breed. At that point when their native intelligence runs smack into their obstinacy, you can have a little tyrant on your hands with the full-throated hound voice to convey his opinion about everything.

We asked **Gary Clacher of Misken Beagles** how the training of a Beagle compares to other breeds.

"Beagles have a bad reputation for being hard to train, but if you put the hard work in early it certainly pays off. Being more food driven than probably any other dog, a pocketful of biscuits is a great incentive when training a youngster! However, I have learned the hard way that no matter how well trained a dog may be, when a Beagle's nose gets onto the trail of whatever, the ears switch off. Once in hunting mode — forget it, for the vast majority of Beagles. I only let mine off-lead in fenced areas.

"A few years back I had four off-lead in one of the 'safe zones,' which is an area of around 5 acres completely surrounded with deer fence. My old girl of 11 years disappeared and, following her tracks, came to a knocked down fence panel and little tell-tale paw prints. After a couple of hours, I went home and made 'wanted posters' and stuck them everywhere around the woods. Five hours later I got a phone call from a dog walker saying she'd spotted a Beagle. I was back there in a flash just in time to see a deer break cover and run across our path — followed five seconds later by our old one with nose to the ground, tail in the air, and singing the song of the Beagle in pursuit. She came back to us both very sheepish and very tired."

Beagles are good watch dogs. They will alert you to the presence of strangers, but will then warm up quickly when they see you're okay with the visitor. If you do get involved in a situation where your dog is the one acting out toward another animal with any of the typical threat displays like snapping, lunging, pushing, barking, or baring its teeth, you need to be the one who takes charge.

When it comes to dog training, there are several different methods to choose from. For Beagles, however, positive reinforcement training is the most effective. With this type of training you reward your dog for performing desired behaviors and, in doing so, reinforce that behavior. If your dog gets a treat for sitting when you tell him to sit, he will be more likely to repeat that behavior in the future.

Beagles have an eager-to-please attitude that will help to speed up the process. The key to training your Beagle effectively is to make things as simple as possible and to make sure that your dog understands what you want him to do. If you do not consistently reward your Beagle for performing the desired behavior during the early stages of training, he may not learn which behavior it is that you want or he might become frustrated.

Introduce him to new sights, sounds, people, and places. Let him interact with other dogs in a controlled environment. There, the dog is safe to deal with fear and timidity without blustering self-defense postures. You'll get a better-mannered dog and a greater understanding of how to guide your pet's future interactions.

Previously, I discussed leash training, which is crucial for successful public outings. Rather than avoiding areas with other people and dogs, your goal is to be able to take your dog to such places without incident.

Beagles thrive on interaction with their humans and can be happily engaged in interesting public places like parks, walking trails, or beaches that are full of new sights, sounds, and smells. Contrary to what some people think, well-managed outings in varied environments help to create confidence in your dog.

A Beagle will "shut down" with any harsh correction, so having a fun and positive training session is a must — as well as very good treats (mine like liver or chicken)!

Keep training sessions short and fun, and end with a game or a special toy. It is OK to be silly with a Beagle, —they enjoy it!! A high pitch to your voice and lots of love is appreciated. I say '"YES" when they do something right and give an immediate treat.

If you do use a leash, try using a separate leash for training and they will learn to tell the difference between this and a regular walking leash. Most of all, you will need patience and a sense of humor to train a Beagle.

Responsible dog owners are attentive to the behavior of their own dog and to what's going on around them. They praise good behavior, but accept responsibility for anticipating potential clashes.

Obedience training is essential to have a well-behaved Beagle that will respond to your commands regardless of the situation. A training class exposes your puppy new sights, sounds, people, and places. There he can interact with other dogs in a controlled environment and deal safely with any feelings of fear and timidity or territoriality and dominance. The time and effort are well worth it to get a better-mannered dog and a greater understanding of how to guide your pet's future interactions.

Dog Whispering

Many people can be confused when they need professional help with their dog because for many years, if you needed help with your dog,

you contacted a "dog trainer" or took your dog to "puppy classes," where your dog would learn how to sit or stay.

The difference between a dog trainer and a dog whisperer would be that a dog trainer teaches a dog how to perform certain tasks, and a dog whisperer alleviates behavior problems by teaching humans what they need to do to keep their particular dog happy.

Often, depending on how soon the guardian has sought help, this can mean that the dog in question has developed some pretty serious issues, such as aggressive barking, lunging, biting, or attacking other dogs, pets, or people.

Dog whispering is often an emotional roller coaster ride for the humans involved that unveils many truths when they finally realize that it has been their actions (or inactions) that have likely caused the unbalanced behavior that their dog is now displaying. Once solutions are provided, the relief for both dog and human can be quite cathartic when they realize that with the correct direction, they can indeed live a happy life with their dog.

All specific methods of training, such as "clicker" training, fall outside of what every dog needs to be happy, because training your dog to respond to a clicker, which you can easily do on your own, and then letting them sleep in your bed, eat from your plate, and any other multitude of things humans allow, are what makes the dog unbalanced and causes behavior problems.

I always say to people, don't wait until you have a severe problem before getting some dog whispering or professional help of some sort, because with the proper training, Man can learn to be dog's best friend.

Don't Reward Bad Behavior

It is very important to recognize that any attention paid to an out-of-control, adolescent puppy, even negative attention, is likely to be exciting and rewarding for your Beagle puppy.

Chasing after a puppy when they have taken something they shouldn't have, picking them up when barking or showing aggression, pushing them off when they jump on other people, or yelling when they refuse to come when called are all forms of attention that can actually be rewarding for most puppies.

It will be your responsibility to provide structure for your puppy, which will include finding acceptable and safe ways to allow your puppy to vent their energy without being destructive or harmful to others.

The worst thing you can do when training your Beagle is to yell at him or use punishment. Positive reinforcement training methods — that is, rewarding your dog for good behavior — are infinitely more effective than negative reinforcement — training by punishment.

It is important when training your Beagle that you do not allow yourself to get frustrated. If you feel yourself starting to get angry, take a break and come back to the training session later. Why is punishment-based training so bad? Think about it this way — your dog should listen to you because he wants to please you, right?

If you train your dog using punishment, he could become fearful of you and that could put a damper on your relationship with him. Do your dog and yourself a favor by using positive reinforcement.

Teaching Basic Commands

When it comes to training your Beagle, you have to start off slowly with the basic commands. The most popular basic commands for dogs include sit, down, stay, and come.

Sit

This is the most basic and one of the most important commands you can teach your Beagle.

1.   Stand in front of your Beagle with a few small treats in your pocket.

2.   Hold one treat in your dominant hand and wave it in front of your Beagle's nose so he gets the scent.

3.   Give the "Sit" command.

4.   Move the treat upward and backward over your Beagle's head so he is forced to raise his head to follow it.

5.   In the process, his bottom will lower to the ground.

6.   As soon as your Beagle's bottom hits the ground, praise him and give him the treat.

7.   Repeat this process several times until your dog gets the hang of it and responds consistently.

Down

After the "Sit" command, "Down" is the next logical command to teach because it is a progression from "Sit."

1.   Kneel in front of your Beagle with a few small treats in your pocket.

2.   Hold one treat in your dominant hand and give your Beagle the "Sit" command.

3.   Reward your Beagle for sitting, then give him the "Down" command.

4.   Quickly move the treat down to the floor between your Beagle's paws.

5.   Your dog will follow the treat and should lie down to retrieve it.

6.   Praise and reward your Beagle when he lies down.

7.   Repeat this process several times until your dog gets the hang of it and responds consistently.

Come

It is very important that your Beagle responds to a "Come" command, because there may come a time when you need to get his attention and call him to your side during a dangerous situation (such as him running around too close to traffic).

1.   Put your Beagle on a short leash and stand in front of him.

2.   Give your Beagle the "Come" command, then quickly take a few steps backward away from him.

3.   Clap your hands and act excited, but do not repeat the "Come" command.

4.   Keep moving backwards in small steps until your Beagle follows and comes to you.

5.   Praise and reward your Beagle and repeat the process.

6.   Over time, you can use a longer leash or take your Beagle off the leash entirely.

7.   You can also start by standing further from your Beagle when you give the "Come" command.

8.   If your Beagle doesn't come to you immediately, you can use the leash to pull him toward you.

Photo Credit: Gary Clacher of Misken Beagles.

Stay

This command is very important because it teaches your Beagle discipline — not only does it teach your Beagle to stay, but it also forces him to listen and pay attention to you.

1.   Find a friend to help you with this training session.

2.   Have your friend hold your Beagle on the leash while you stand in front of the dog.

3.   Give your Beagle the "Sit" command and reward him for responding correctly.

4.   Give your dog the "Stay" command while holding your hand out like a "Stop" sign.

5.   Take a few steps backward away from your dog and pause for 1 to 2 seconds.

6.   Step back toward your Beagle, then praise and reward your dog.

7.   Repeat the process several times, then start moving back a little further before you return to your dog.

Beyond Basic Training

Once your Beagle has a firm grasp on the basics, you can move on to teaching him additional commands. You can also add distractions to the equation to reinforce your dog's mastery of the commands.

The end goal is to ensure that your Beagle responds to your command each and every time — regardless of distractions and anything else he might rather be doing. This is incredibly important, because there may come a time when your dog is in a dangerous situation and if he doesn't respond to your command, he could get hurt.

If you previously conducted your training sessions indoors, you might consider moving them outside where your dog could be distracted by various sights, smells, and sounds.

One thing you might try is to give your dog the Stay command and then toss a toy nearby that will tempt him to break his Stay. Start by tossing the toy at a good distance from him and wait a few seconds before you release him to play. Eventually you will be able to toss a toy right next to your dog without him breaking his Stay until you give him permission to do so.

Incorporating Hand Signals

Teaching your Beagle to respond to hand signals in addition to verbal commands is very useful — you never know when you will be in a situation where your dog might not be able to hear you.

To start out, choose your dominant hand to give the hand signals, and

hold a small treat in that hand while you are training your dog — this will encourage your dog to focus on your hand during training, and it will help to cement the connection between the command and the hand signal.

Photo Credit: Mary Cummings and Sue Nichols of Stone Meadow & The Hounds of Lightfall.

To begin, give your dog the Sit or Down command while holding the treat in your dominant hand and give the appropriate hand signal — for Sit, you might try a closed fist and for Down, you might place your hand flat, parallel to the ground.

When your dog responds correctly, give him the treat. You will need to repeat this process many times in order for your dog to form a connection between both the verbal command and the hand signal with the desired behavior.

Eventually, you can start to remove the verbal command from the equation — use the hand gesture every time, but start to use the verbal command only half the time.

Once your dog gets the hang of this, you should start to remove the food reward from the equation. Continue to give your dog the hand signal for each command, and occasionally use the verbal command just to remind him.

You should start to phase out the food rewards, however, by offering them only half the time. Progressively lessen the use of the food reward, but continue to praise your dog for performing the behavior correctly so he learns to repeat it.

Teaching Distance Commands

In addition to getting your dog to respond to hand signals, it is also useful to teach him to respond to your commands even when you are not directly next to him.

This may come in handy if your dog is running around outside and gets too close to the street — you should be able to give him a Sit or Down command so he stops before he gets into a dangerous situation.

Teaching your dog distance commands is not difficult, but it does require some time and patience.

To start, give your Beagle a brief refresher course of the basic commands while you are standing or kneeling right next to him.

Next, give your dog the Sit and Stay commands, then move a few feet away before you give the Come command.

Repeat this process, increasing the distance between you and your dog before giving him the Come command. Be sure to praise and reward your dog for responding appropriately when he does so.

Once your dog gets the hang of coming on command from a distance, you can start to incorporate other commands. One method of doing so is to teach your dog to sit when you grab his collar. To do so, let your dog wander freely and every once in a while, walk up and grab his collar while giving the Sit command.

After a few repetitions, your dog should begin to respond with a Sit when you grab his collar, even if you do not give the command. Gradually, you can increase the distance from which you come to grab his collar and give him the command.

After your dog starts to respond consistently when you come from a distance to grab his collar, you can start giving the Sit command without moving toward him. It may take your dog a few times to get

the hang of it, so be patient. If your dog doesn't sit right away, calmly walk up to him and repeat the Sit command, but do not grab his collar this time.

Eventually, your dog will get the hang of it, and you can start to practice using other commands like Down and Stay from a distance.

Clicker Training

To help speed up the training process for your Beagle, you might want to look into clicker training. Clicker training is a version of positive reinforcement training.

When it comes to training your Beagle, you are going to be most successful if you maintain consistency. Unless you are very clear with your dog about what your expectations are, he may simply decide not to follow your commands.

A simple way to achieve consistency in training your Beagle is to use the principles of clicker training. This involves using a small handheld device that makes a clicking noise when you press it between your fingers.

Clicker training is based on the theory of operant conditioning, which helps your dog to make the connection between the desired behavior and the offering of a reward.

Beagles have a natural desire to please, so if they learn that a certain behavior earns your approval, they will be eager to repeat it — this is a great way to help your dog quickly identify the particular behavior you want him to repeat.

All you have to do is give your Beagle a command and, as soon as he performs the behavior, you use the clicker. After you use the clicker, give your dog the reward as you would with any form of positive reinforcement training.

You should only use the clicker for the first few times to make sure that your Beagle doesn't become dependent on the sound to perform the behavior.

Use food rewards during the early stages of training for positive reinforcement, but phase them out after your Beagle gets the hang of each command.

Some of the benefits of clicker training include:

• Very easy to implement — all you need is the clicker.

• Helps your dog form a connection between the command and the desired behavior more quickly.

• You only need to use the clicker until your dog makes the connection, then you can stop.

• May help to keep your dog's attention more effectively if he hears the noise.

Clicker training is just one method of positive reinforcement training that you can consider for training your Beagle. No matter what method you choose, it is important that you maintain consistency and always praise and reward your dog for responding to your commands correctly so he learns to repeat the behavior.

First Tricks

When teaching your Beagle their first tricks, in order to give them extra incentive, find a small treat that they would do anything to get, and give the treat as a reward to help solidify a good performance.

Most dogs will be extra attentive during training sessions when they know that they will be rewarded with their favorite treats.

If your Beagle is less than six months old when you begin teaching them tricks, keep your training sessions short (no more than 5 or 10 minutes) and make the sessions lots of fun. As your Beagle becomes an adult, you can extend your sessions because they will be able to maintain their focus for longer periods of time.

Playing Dead

Once your Beagle knows the command to "lie down," which should be one of the basic obedience commands he learns at "school," getting him to "play dead" is simple.

Once the dog is lying down, hold a treat in front of your pet close enough for him to smell it. Move the treat in circles toward the floor giving your Beagle the command, "Play Dead."

The motion should encourage the dog to roll over on his back. As soon as he achieves the correct position, praise him and give him the treat. Beagles love treats so much, it won't take your pet long to put it all together and execute the maneuver on command.

Shake a Paw

Who doesn't love a dog who knows how to shake a paw? This is one of the easiest tricks to teach your Beagle.

Practice every day until they are 100% reliable with this trick, and then it will be time to add another trick to their repertoire.

Most dogs are naturally either right or left pawed. If you know which paw your dog favors, ask them to shake this paw.

Find a quiet place to practice, without noisy distractions or other pets, and stand or sit in front of your dog. Place them in the sitting position and hold a treat in your left hand.

Say the command "Shake" while putting your right hand behind their left or right paw and pulling the paw gently toward yourself until you are holding their paw in your hand. Immediately praise them and give them the treat.

Most dogs will learn the "Shake" trick very quickly, and in no time at all, once you put out your hand, your Beagle will immediately lift their paw and put it into your hand without your assistance or any verbal cue.

Give Me Five

The next trick after "Shake" should be "High Five." Teach this sequence the same way, but when you hold out your hand to shake, move your hand up and touch your dog's paw saying, "High five!." It may take a few tries, but by this time your Beagle will be getting the idea that if he learns his lessons, he gets his treat.

This set of four tricks is a good example of using one behavior to build to another. Almost any dog can be taught to perform basic tricks, but don't lose sight of the fact that you are dealing with an individual personality. You may have a Beagle that would rather chase his chew toys than learn "routines." Get to know what your dog enjoys doing and follow his lead to build his unique set of tricks.

Roll Over

You will find that just like your Beagle is naturally either right or left pawed, that they will also naturally want to roll to either the right or the left side.

Take advantage of this by asking your dog to roll to the side they naturally prefer. Sit with your dog on the floor and put them in a lying down position.

Hold a treat in your hand and place it close to their nose without allowing them to grab it, and while they are in the lying position, move the treat to the right or left side of their head so that they have to roll over to get to it.

You will quickly see which side they want to naturally roll to; once you see this, move the treat to that side. Once they roll over to that side, immediately give them the treat and praise them.

Photo Credit: Susie Arden of Madika Beagles.

You can say the verbal cue "Over" while you demonstrate the hand signal motion (moving your right hand in a half circular motion) from one side of their head to the other.

Sit Pretty

While this trick is a little more complicated, and most dogs pick up on it very quickly, remember that this trick requires balance, and every dog is different, so always exercise patience.

Find a quiet space with few distractions and sit or stand in front of your dog and ask them to "Sit."

Have a treat nearby (on a countertop or table) and when they sit, use both of your hands to lift up their front paws into the sitting pretty position, while saying the command "Sit Pretty." Help them balance in this position while you praise them and give them the treat.

Once your Beagle can do the balancing part of the trick quite easily without your help, sit or stand in front of your dog while asking them to "Sit Pretty" and hold the treat above their head, at the level their nose would be when they sit pretty.

If they attempt to stand on their back legs to get the treat, you may be holding the treat too high, which will encourage them to stand up on their back legs to reach it. Go back to the first step and put them back into the "Sit" position, and again lift their paws while their backside remains on the floor.

The hand signal for "Sit Pretty" is a straight arm held over your dog's head with a closed fist. Place your Beagle beside a wall when first teaching this trick so that they can use the wall to help their balance.

A young Beagle puppy should be able to easily learn these basic tricks before they are six months old, and when you are patient and make your training sessions short and fun for your dog, they will be eager to learn more.

Excessive Jumping

Beagles are excellent climbers and have no compunction about making leaps that will put your heart in your throat if you're watching. Pair that with their excellent noses and insatiable curiosity, and your real problem with jumping may involve leaps onto the table to snag the Sunday pot roast.

If you do have a dog that is bored and suffering from anxiety, his hyperactivity will kick in and he may begin to jump up on people. Allowing any dog to jump in this fashion is a serious mistake. Jumping is one of the most undesirable of all traits in a companion canine. Many people are afraid of dogs, and find spontaneous jumping threatening.

Don't assume that excessive jumping is an expression of friendliness. All too often it's a case of a dominant dog asserting his authority and saying, "I don't respect you." Dogs that know their proper place in the "pack" don't jump on more dominant dogs — or on more dominant humans! A jumper sees himself as the "top dog" in all situations.

As the dog's master, you must enforce the "no jumping" rule. Anything else will only confuse your pet. Dogs have a keen perception of space. Rather than retreating from a jumping dog, step sideways and forward, taking back your space that he is trying to claim.

You are not trying to knock your dog down, but he may careen into you and fall anyway. Remain casual and calm. Take slow, deliberate motions and protect the "bubble" around your body. Your dog won't be expecting this action from you, and won't enjoy it.

After several failed jumps the dog will lose interest when his dominant message is no longer getting across.

It is important to praise him when he does have all four feet on the ground. Rewarding good behavior is often forgotten.

TIPS FROM EXPERT BREEDERS: Let's begin by saying that you have to establish right away who the pack leader is. This is KEY in all aspects of owning an obedient, respectful dog. Please keep in mind that dogs understand dog language. If a momma dog has an issue with her young, she would never tolerate it. If she sees something she doesn't like, she will move the puppy in a calm assertive manner, out of the way. She uses her body to teach boundaries. You can use yours too. When you have a dog that habitually jumps up, he/she is establishing that they are your pack leader. Gain control of this by teaching your dog simple commands. This is imperative to having a great, social member of society. When you come in and you are greeted by your dog, make him sit before being petted. If he jumps on you, softly meet him/her with a raised knee, a firm "OFF" and follow with the command "SIT." Praise your dog when you get the desired results. You must be consistent!! Remember, you also must establish from the beginning (puppy stage) that you are the pack leader. A pack leader never negotiates. If you are inconsistent it could lead to role reversal, creating a dog that is confused, nervous, anxious, and one that may never be house trainable. Think like a dog and you will be very successful at being TOP DOG!

Photo Credit: Carol and Lori Norman of Lokavi Beagles.

Barking Behavior

You'll never have a completely quiet Beagle. He's built to use his voice and his repertoire extends far beyond a simple bark and well into the range of impressive and expressive baying and howling. A Beagle in all his full-throated glory can raise the roof and drive the neighbor's insane.

In an apartment setting, your vocal pet can easily get you tossed out on your ear and in any residential setting, be the cause of an out and out neighbor war. The answer to problem barking in Beagles is usually more exercise and intellectual stimulation, but if these simple solutions don't work, you may need the help of an expert to figure out what is setting your dog off.

Your Beagle may bark for the following reasons:

Boredom — Being left alone for long periods of time causes sadness.

Fear — They may sense a threat such as another animal.

Greeting — They love to greet visitors, or perhaps on a walk they want to communicate with another dog. This would usually be accompanied with a wagging tail and maybe jumping up.

Getting Attention — He may need to go outside to go to the toilet, or maybe he wants attention from you or food.

So what can you do when you have an issue?

1. Nip it in the bud by dealing with barking problems as quickly as possible before it escalates.

2. Fence your garden or yard with solid fencing so he feels safer and less threatened.

3. Ignore your Beagle until he stops barking. You don't want him thinking he can just bark and get what he wants, or he will only keep repeating the behavior.

4. If he barks while you're out and the neighbors complain, he is bored. Don't leave him as long; get someone to come in and play with him or leave toys that occupy him.

5. As with all problem behaviors, address barking with patience and consistency. Don't shout and get angry — he will bark even louder.

6. You can feed him a treat AFTER as a reward but never when he is barking, otherwise he will start to bark to get a treat!

7. For real problem barkers, humane bark collars can teach the dog through negative reinforcement. These collars release a harmless spray of citronella into the dog's nose in response to vibrations in the throat. The system, though somewhat expensive at $100 / £60, works in almost all cases.

TIPS FROM EXPERT BREEDERS: This is a natural way of communication for our pets. It is important that you are always the pack leader. Every habit picked up by dogs can be easily corrected if you maintain this status early on. It is the language that dogs can understand and relate to. A lot of times, excess barking is a result of pent up or excess energy. Take lots of time to interact with your dog and the problems that arise from a frustrated dog will be fewer. When a dog is barking, divert their attention. Hopefully you have been consistent in your interaction with your dog and you have established some simple commands. If you haven't, this is a good place to start.

Teach sit, down, stay, off, and come/recall. Once you have these commands successfully instilled in your dog, the command "QUIET" will be a lot easier. The use of a leash if your dog is outside or inside is very helpful. You can grab the leash and divert his/her attention while they are barking by grabbing the leash and redirecting their attention to you with a command of "NO BARK" or "Quiet," whichever you prefer. I can't stress enough how consistency is key, along with having already established your alpha status. If you are unsuccessful at teaching these commands, please seek the advice of a professional.

Ruth Darlene Stewart of Aladar Beagles: "The personality of the dog determines the amount of barking, potentially. If you take a dog with the genetic potential to bark and put him in a stimulating environment with other barkers — well guess what, he will bark. Other puppies in that same litter may not be so prone to bark. In each of my litters there seems to be a loud-mouth. Often enough that loud-mouth is the dominant dog. Is this nature's way of the dog protecting his pack?

"No matter what, barkers can be annoying. First, consider that the dog may be bored or want more attention. Do you spend time with your dog? The next time your dog starts barking, see if there is definite stimulus and if not, try spending time with the dog. My barkers tend to bark when there are other strange dogs near 'their' fence or when I am working with another one of my dogs. Most dogs will bark when the owner comes home, but this is a happy bark and should stop as soon as you give the dogs a hello cuddle. I do have one dog that regardless of what I tried he barked the most irritating bark. I have solved his problem with an electronic bark collar. With repetitive barking he gets a warning beep and then if he barks again, he gets a mild shock. It has worked wonders, and when he does not have it on he barks, freely."

Chasing

If you don't want a dog that will relentlessly chase a scent and decide in a heartbeat that a smaller animal is his "quarry," don't get a Beagle. This is the kind of behavior the breed is literally engineered for. It's in their blood to the point that a Beagle literally cannot ignore a scent trail.

In order to keep your Beagle safe from his own instincts, you must keep him leashed at all times when he is not in a secure area. A Beagle on a scent will not look left or right and can easily run into traffic in a busy urban area. Even if your dog does survive those kinds of perils, Beagles are notorious for refusing to come when they are called. They can get lost easily and quickly.

Ruth Darlene Stewart of Aladar Beagles: "Puppies love to play chase and often the human animal is the one doing the chasing. Start with young puppies and teach them that when they run away, you do not chase. Instead, turn and walk a few paces away, squat or sit down and IGNORE the puppy. The puppy will usually come to you to play. Let the puppy touch you and then you scratch, pat, and cuddle the puppy. Giving a treat at this time will also help teach the puppy not to run away. Gradually, as the puppy grows, start using 'come' to begin teaching this command."

Chewing

Beagles are associated with the full range of destructive behaviors typical of separation anxiety, including chewing. This is a natural behavior in dogs, but if left undirected, a Beagle with a fetish for chewing is capable of causing unbelievable levels of mayhem in your home.

Again, the answer is probably a matter of getting your dog out of the house more. If I sound like a broken record, I mean to. Don't get a Beagle if you're not prepared for his real physical and emotional need for exercise and interesting activities.

Normal chewing relieves anxiety, keeps their jaws strong and their teeth clean. However, excessive chewing indicates some combination of anxiety or boredom. Make sure you are giving your Beagle plenty of physical and mental stimulation by taking him to the dog park, playing games such as fetch, or enrolling him in activities such as agility training.

Puppies go through a teething stage like human babies where they lose their baby teeth and experience pain as their adult teeth grow through. This should be done with by about twelve months, but before then you can still channel your puppy's urge to chew in the right direction. Make sure your dog has proper chew toys that exist to be destroyed! Keep things interesting by buying new ones every so often.

Yes, you can give him a bone, but only natural bones that are sold specifically for chewing, because cooked bones can splinter and seriously injure him.

If you catch your pet chewing on a forbidden object, reprimand (I don't mean punish) him and take the item away. Immediately substitute an appropriate chew toy and if you chose to, reward him with attention or a treat.

You can buy chewing deterrents such as Grannick's Bitter Apple spray, which you spray on all objects that you don't want your dog to chew. Reapply the deterrent every day for two to four weeks.

TIPS FROM EXPERT BREEDERS: We have to be mindful of the fact that from 3–8 weeks puppies are getting their deciduous teeth. Those teeth will then be replaced by their permanent teeth from 4-6 months. These are the times that chewing is at its most painful. Their gums are very irritated, and chewing is their natural instinct at this time. This can lead to a long-standing problem, however, if you do not get it under control. Please always rule out any potential medical problem causing the excess chewing. Always maintain alpha dog status. This will help with them chewing your belongings. Puppy proof your home. Do not let puppy have free access to your home, and never unsupervised.

Provide acceptable chew items, like raw bones, antlers, and perhaps a Kong with organic peanut butter in it. Never feed cooked bones or rawhide, and always supervise your dog when he has something to chew on. Deter your dog from chewing on unacceptable items with replacement of acceptable things. Dogs benefit greatly from exercise. A dog that is stimulated with exercise is usually one that will rest when play time or walk time is over.

Ruth Darlene Stewart of Aladar Beagles: "Never give a puppy a shoe to chew on — he will always think shoes are to chew on and will not know the difference between the cheap shoes and the expensive shoes. All puppies will chew, just like human babies — teething means chewing."

Stacey Burrows of Summerlily Beagles: "I give a teething puppy carrot batons to chew into; it's cool and soothing on the gums. I also give my adult Beagles carrots as treats, which they of course love!

"If you find your puppy chewing on something he shouldn't, say 'give' and take it away from him gently. Always give your puppy the proper chew toy in trade, telling him 'take' and then 'good boy' after he has the 'right' toy in his mouth. If he resists giving you the 'bad' toy, slowly put pressure at the back of the jaw where the upper and lower teeth meet. Make sure you press with the skin of the cheek between your fingers and his teeth. That way if he bites down he is actually hurting himself. Remember to give the command 'give' and praise him after he has taken the trade toy."

Digging

Digging is such a serious and common problem with Beagles. This breed absolutely must not be left unobserved in a fenced backyard. While this kind of behavior may indicate fear, anxiety, and/or boredom, it's also highly likely the dog smells something on the other side of the fence he is bound and determined to investigate.

Digging is a difficult behavior to stop with any breed and all but impossible to curb in a Beagle. An out-of-control digger in the house can destroy your sofa or some other piece of furniture. If you cannot be home during the day to give your Beagle the interaction he craves, enroll your pet in a dog daycare facility. He'll love going to "work" every day and you'll be saved walking into a wrecked house.

Ruth Darlene Stewart of Aladar Beagles: "Most diggers do so for specific reasons. Again, try thinking like a dog. Is your dog digging to make a cool bed, chasing a bug, burying a toy, or because of boredom? You cannot put a puppy or dog into the backyard and not spend quality time with them. They will find ways to entertain themselves and your freshly planted flower garden (your smell will be strongest there) will be just too tempting! Mole crickets seem to be my undoing. Regardless of how much mole cricket poison I use, I cannot get rid of them! My dogs are the best mole cricket chasers resulting in small round ankle-getting holes each spring. Also, some dogs will dig to get out. Again, dogs will get bored and they are by instinct pack animals. If there are other dogs to go play with and your dog does not get enough attention from YOU, then he will seek out other pack members."

Begging

Begging is also a constant problem with a Beagle, but they're so athletic, they take their chow hound tendencies a step farther and actively go after any forbidden food they can reach. Don't be at all surprised if you walk in the kitchen to find your Beagle on the counter. The dining room table is no stretch for his abilities. Never leave food within a Beagle's reach or it will be gone.

The breed is highly susceptible to weight gain, and when they're not outright stealing food, they're quite good at using their charms to get what they want. A Beagle can easily sag his features into the trademark sad hound dog expression, augmented with liquid, pleading eyes and a head cocked questioningly to the side at just the right moment.

Stay strong! Obesity can be life-threatening. Make "people" food off limits from day one. If your pet becomes a serious beggar, confine him to another part of the house during meal times. If you can't ignore a set of pleading eyes imploring you to share your dinner, you're the real problem!

Biting

Beagles are not known to be problem biters, but any dog will bite if he is reacting out of pain or fear. Biting is a primary means of defense. Use socialization, obedience training, and stern corrections to control a puppy's playful nips.

With their littermates, your Beagle would have learned about bite inhibition, which is a dog's ability to control the pressure he uses when biting so that he doesn't cause pain or harm. When puppies are playing, if they bite too hard the other puppy will yelp or run away, which teaches the puppy not to bite so hard. This would have curbed the rough play, and this technique can be used when this nipping becomes painful or dangerous to you.

If your Beagle puppy has a tendency to bite you a little harder than you think he should, you can teach him bite inhibition yourself. When playing with your puppy if he bites you, you should say "Ouch!" in a calm tone and gently remove your hand from his mouth to imitate the reaction, as if from a sibling in the pack. After you do, stop paying attention to the puppy for a few seconds before resuming play. It may also be helpful for you to give your puppy a chew toy after removing your hand, so he learns what he is and is not allowed to chew on.

Obviously, any dog will bite if he is reacting out of pain or fear. Biting is a dog's primary means of defense. Use socialization, obedience training, and stern corrections to control a puppy's playful nips. If an adult dog displays biting behavior, it is imperative to get to the bottom of the biting. Have the dog evaluated for a health problem and work with a professional trainer.

Photo Credit: Samantha Goldberg of Molesend Beagles.

Ruth Darlene Stewart of Aladar Beagles: "It is natural for puppies to bite and chew on one another; therefore, they will playfully do this to their human playmates. It is ok for a puppy to mouth your hand, but biting is not accepted. Think like a puppy playmate. When a puppy bites another too hard, the bitten puppy quits playing. If your puppy bites too hard scream 'OWWWW' and turn away. Ignore the puppy. When the puppy plays nicely always praise him. (This method will only work if the puppy has been left with its littermates long enough to learn this lesson — that is why you should not buy a puppy before 8 weeks of age.)

"Teach your children this and never allow or encourage children to hit the puppy. The puppy will naturally want to 'catch' the moving hand, and a future biter may be in the beginning stages. The same goes for a puppy that chases and bites. Do not run from the puppy, stop — tell him no and ignore him. Running from the puppy is fun to the puppy.

You can teach the puppy to follow by walking calmly, calling his name, and giving a treat. When giving a puppy a treat, always say 'easy' and never jerk the food away. Encourage your puppy to take food from your hand from the beginning. Hopefully, the breeder has already started hand feeding treats at weaning."

Dealing with Copraphagia

Copraphagia is when dogs eat feces, either their own or that of another animal. While we may be appalled at this, it is actually quite common in dogs. The problem is that nobody really seems to know why this happens. Reasons speculated upon include a lack of nutrition in their diet, being left alone, or learned behavior from their time in the litter.

Mostly they will grow out of this, but how can we discourage it?

1. Clean up after him as soon as he has eliminated.

2. Keep him stimulated with chew toys and games and don't leave him alone for long periods.

3. Review his diet — Vitamin-B deficiency is a key suspect, but it could be another nutrient he is lacking.

You could feed certain foods that are expelled and smell disgusting to him, so he avoids eating them. These include parsley and courgettes/zucchinis.

Ruth Darlene Stewart of Aladar Beagles: "Stool eating is one of the major drawbacks to owning a Beagle, although not all do this and there are products on the market to help break this habit. I believe it is due to their strong nose and the rich food we feed them. I have had puppies start this habit as soon as they were started on commercial dog food. Check with your veterinarian for his/her suggestions. There are numerous commercial products that might help curb or stop this problem."

Chapter 11 — Beagle Health

You are your Beagle's primary healthcare provider. You will know what is "normal" for your dog. Yours will be the best sense that something is "wrong" even when there is no obvious injury or illness. The more you understand preventive healthcare, the better you will care for your Beagle throughout his life.

Photo Credit: Diana Brown of Raimex Beagles.

Sam Goldberg of BeagleHealth.info: "As a general rule the Beagle is a moderately built healthy breed without any conformational issues seen in some breeds. There are some genetic tests that breeders are recommended to check for and these are listed on the U.K. Beagle Site http://www.beaglehealth.info. The U.K. Kennel Club supports a Breed Health Coordinator who is appointed by each breed. This person monitors the health of the breed and helps with queries and problems relating to their breed. This is not a substitute for your vet if your dog is ill but someone who supports and helps with advice when needed."

Your Veterinarian Is Your Partner

Working with a qualified veterinarian is critical to long-term and comprehensive healthcare. If you do not already have a vet, ask your breeder for a recommendation. If you purchased your pet outside your area, contact your local dog club and ask for referrals.

Make an appointment to tour the clinic and meet the vet. Be clear about the purpose of your visit and don't waste anyone's time! Go in with a set of prepared questions. Be sure to cover the following points:

- How long has this practice been in operation?
- How many vets are on staff?
- Are any of your doctors specialists?
- If not, to which doctors do you refer patients?
- What are your regular business hours?
- Do you recommend a specific emergency clinic?
- Do you have emergency hours?
- What specific medical services do you offer?
- Do you offer grooming services?
- Do you currently treat any Beagles?
- May I have an estimated schedule of fees?

Pay attention to all aspects of your visit, including how the facilities appear, and the demeanor of the staff. Things to look for include:

- how the staff interacts with clients
- the degree of organization or lack thereof
- indications of engagement with the clientele (office bulletin board, cards and photos displayed, etc.)
- quality of all visible equipment
- cleanliness and orderliness of the waiting area and back rooms
- prominent display of doctors' qualifications

These are only some suggestions. Go with your "gut." If the clinic and staff seems to "feel" right to you, trust your instincts. If not, no matter how well-appointed the practice may appear to be, visit more clinics before making a decision.

When you are comfortable with a vet practice, schedule a second visit to include your Beagle puppy. Bring all the dog's medical records. Be ready to discuss completing vaccinations.

Routine exam procedures include temperature and a check of heart and lung function with a stethoscope. The vet will weigh and measure the puppy. These baseline numbers will help chart growth and physical progress. If you have specific questions, prepare them in advance.

BE AWARE: While the majority of veterinary organizations are well-meaning, they are businesses that need to make a profit, much of which can be from annual re-vaccinations and selling processed foods, both of which may not necessarily be in the best interests of your Beagle.

Spaying and Neutering

Most reputable Beagle sales are conducted by way of spay/neuter contracts stipulating that spaying or neutering is to be completed after the puppy has reached sexual maturity.

Females can get pregnant in old age — they don't go through a menopause. Spaying is the removal of her ovaries and womb (uterus).

Neutering is the removal of the male's testicles, also known as castration, in what is a routine operation. Yes, of course he will feel tender and slightly sore, but this will last only a few days.

Ask yourself, why wouldn't you have these procedures done unless of course you are planning to breed? Don't be swayed by popular misconceptions (myths) such as the operation will subdue or permanently affect his character and personality, or that the dog will gain weight. Remember that dogs are not humans; their need for sex is purely physical, caused by hormones that when removed will mean your dog does not desire or miss sex.

It is very important that spay/neuter procedures are done **after sexual maturity** because there is ongoing emotional maturing that needs to take place. This maturation happens during the final phase of puppy adolescence (usually 12 months old) and helps to achieve healthy, balanced adult Beagle behavior. Sexual maturity happens after a first menstrual cycle, often referred to as being "in heat" or "in season," and takes place in the bitch puppy and after the male dog is capable of having the ability to sire pups.

A female Beagle will have her menstrual cycle every 6 or 8 months on average, and this lasts usually 12–21 days. Her hormones will be raging, and through a sense of smell hundreds of times more powerful than ours, the male dogs from miles around will be on alert. You will notice some bleeding (spotting). This is perfectly normal.

Sam Goldberg of BeagleHealth.info: "It is recommended that a bitch has a season before neutering to ensure maturity and reduce issues such as urinary incontinence in later years."

Photo Credit: Gary Clacher of Misken Beagles.

Spay and neuter procedures may also carry some health and behavioral benefits:

1. Neutering reduces the risk of prostatic disease or perianal tumors in male dogs.

2. The surgery may also lessen aggressive behaviors, territorial urine marking, and inappropriate mounting.

3. Spayed females have a diminished risk for breast cancer and no prospect of uterine or ovarian cancer.

4. There is no possibility of an unplanned or unwanted litter.

5.   There are no mood swings related to hormones or issues (such as mess) around the bitch coming into season.

Vaccinations

If your Beagle puppy is not immunized, then he is at risk from potentially fatal canine diseases because he has no protection. Contact with other dogs could occur at parks or at the vet's, so be very careful until he has received his first vaccinations. After birth, puppies receive immunity to many diseases from their mother's milk (this is called colostrum), but as they mature, this immunity fades.

Without immunization, your pup won't be covered under any pet insurance policy you may have taken out.

To give a balanced view, I will also point out that some breeders believe some Beagles are **'over-vaccinated'** and while very rare, there is the possibility of a reaction to the vaccine too.

A minor reaction could affect your Beagle in ways such as making them sleepy, sneeze, irritable, and especially sore or developing a lump where injected. These should resolve in a few days.

A more severe reaction requiring immediate treatment would include vomiting, diarrhea, seizures, and a hypersensitivity reaction similar to that of a human anaphylactic reaction.

So what are the worst threats? There are two deadly threats that are the main focus of the initial vaccinations — distemper and parvovirus.

Distemper causes flu-like symptoms initially and progresses to severe painful neurological symptoms such as seizures and often ends in death. The virus is airborne so can be caught if your puppy comes into close proximity of an infected dog.

Parvovirus causes diarrhea and vomiting, often ending in death. The virus can be present in grass or on other surfaces for years.

A puppy's recommended vaccinations begin at 6–7 weeks of age. The most common combination vaccine given is known as **DHPP**. The initials refer to the diseases included in the vaccine — Distemper, Hepatitis, Parvo, and Parainfluenza.

Some vets may also include protection against Coronavirus and the bacteria Leptospirosis at the same time. The first injection thereby protects him from a number of diseases in one go.

In the U.K., this first vaccinations tends to include: Distemper, Canine Parvovirus (Parvo), Infectious Canine Hepatitis (Adenovirus), Leptospirosis, and Kennel Cough (Bordetella).

Why the differences? Canine Coronavirus is a relatively new vaccine and so is not offered as standard in every veterinary practice in the U.K. Rabies is considered to have been eliminated within the U.K., however, if you plan to take your dog out of the country, you will require a pet passport and then they must be vaccinated against rabies.

Recommended boosters occur at 9, 12, and 16 weeks. In some geographical regions in the U.S., a vaccine for Lyme disease (typically in forested areas) starts at 16 weeks with a booster at 18 weeks.

The rabies vaccination is administered at 12–16 weeks and yearly for life thereafter, although many states allow 3 years between rabies vaccinations.

Most vaccinations are administered by means of an injection, although kennel cough is usually administered using a nasal spray.

Once this initial schedule has been completed, the debate opens up over the frequency of boosters. General practice is to give a distemper/parvo booster a year after the completion of their puppy series. After that, it depends on the individual vet, but usually a booster takes place every three years after the completion of the initial puppy series.

Once your puppy has had their second set of vaccines, they should be safe to go into the outside world and play with other dogs.

Some of our breeders are in favor of a titer test. This is a straightforward blood test that measures a dog's antibodies to vaccine viruses. Titers accurately assess protection against the core diseases in dogs, enabling veterinarians to judge whether a booster vaccination is really necessary.

TIP: On vaccinations, I would suggest people need to speak with their vets about local requirements, but be mindful of the latest World Small Animal Veterinary Association (WSAVA) advice, which has moved away from "annual boosters" for everything. Its membership is made up of global veterinary organizations: http://www.wsava.org/

Evaluating for Worms

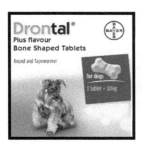

Puppies purchased from a breeder are almost always parasite-free, because puppies are given their first dose of worming medication at around two weeks old, then again at five and eight weeks, before they leave the litter.

This is another reason to make sure you buy from a reputable breeder and not someone who doesn't know what they are doing. Worms are more common in rescue dogs, strays, and from "backyard breeders."

I have talked about taking your Beagle to the vet within days of your purchase to get him health checked. A worm test is usually done then. These tests are important because some parasites, like tapeworms, may be life-threatening. Your vet will need a fecal sample for this purpose.

The main types of worms affecting puppies are **roundworm** and **tapeworm**. Roundworms appear as small white granules around the anus. Other types of worms can only be seen through a microscope.

If the puppy tests positive, the standard treatment is a deworming agent with a follow-up dose in 10 days. Most vets recommend worming a puppy once a month until he is six months old, and then around every two or three months.

Dangers to you: Roundworm can pass from a puppy to humans, in the most severe cases causing blindness or miscarriage in women. Make sure you wash your hands immediately after handling your puppy.

Heartworms

Heartworm (Dirofilaria Immitis) is only present in certain parts of the world (usually the warmer ones), as it is dependent on the mosquitoes that transmit it through their bites. They are thin, long parasites that infest the muscles of the heart, where they block blood vessels and cause bleeding. Their presence can lead to heart failure and death.

Coughing and fainting, as well as an intolerance to exercise, are all symptoms of heartworm. Discuss heartworm prevention with your vet and decide on the best course of action to keep your pet safe.

There is another worm called **Angiostrongylus** (also known as the French heartworm or lungworm), which is carried by slugs and snails. Dogs can be infected by eating them or licking at the trails. The worm can damage the lungs or lodge in the heart, as well as causing clotting disorders.

Warning Signs of Illness in Your Beagle

Often the signs of serious illness are subtle. Trust your instincts. If you think something is wrong, do not hesitate to consult with your vet.

- excessive and unexplained drooling
- excessive consumption of water and increased urination
- changes in appetite leading to weight gain or loss
- marked change in levels of activity
- disinterest in favorite activities
- stiffness and difficulty standing or climbing stairs
- sleeping more than normal
- shaking of the head
- any sores, lumps, or growths
- dry, red, or cloudy eyes

Diarrhea

Beagle puppies, like all small dogs, are subject to digestive upsets. Puppies just will get into things they shouldn't, like human food or even the garbage. Diarrhea from these causes resolves within 24 hours.

During that time, the puppy should have only small portions of dry food and no treats. Give the dog lots of fresh, clean water to guard against dehydration. If the loose, watery stools are still present after 24 hours, take your Beagle to the vet.

The same period of watchful waiting applies for adult dogs. If episodic diarrhea becomes chronic, take a good look at your pet's diet. Chances are good that the dog is getting too much rich, fatty food and needs less fat and protein. Some dogs also do better eating small amounts of food several times a day rather than having 2–3 larger meals.

Allergy testing can identify the causes of some cases of diarrhea. Many small dogs are allergic to chicken and turkey. A change in diet resolves their gastrointestinal upset immediately. Diets based on rabbit or duck are often used for dogs with such intolerances.

Either bacteria or a virus can cause diarrhea, which accompanies fever and vomiting. Parasites, in particular tapeworms and roundworms, may also be to blame.

Understanding Vomiting

Dietary changes or the puppy "getting into something" can also cause vomiting. Again, this should resolve within 24 hours. If the dog tries to vomit but can't bring anything up, vomits blood, or can't keep water down, take your pet to the vet immediately.

Many Beagle owners are concerned about their dogs not eating when their stomach is upset, but the real, main issue in this case is not drinking. Dehydration from vomiting can be fatal. It is possible that your dog may need intravenous fluids.

When your dog is vomiting, always have a good look around to identify what, if anything, the dog may have chewed and swallowed. This can be a huge benefit in targeting appropriate treatment.

Other potential culprits include: hookworm, roundworm, pancreatitis, diabetes, thyroid disease, kidney disease, liver disease, or a physical blockage.

How to Treat Vomiting

If your Beagle seems normal after it has vomited once or even twice, you can use the following treatment in the house as a practical solution.

1. At least for a period of 6 to 8 hours, make sure that your dog has no contact with all sources of food and water.

2. If during this period you see no signs of vomiting, you can allow your dog to have some water. Gradually increase the amount of water if your dog is able to hold the water down.

3. Wait for another 12 hours after allowing him to drink. If there is still

no vomiting, you can start offering a small meal such as plain boiled and deboned chicken meat with white rice. If he eats and doesn't vomit, you can opt to give a bigger meal. Continue observing for a day or two as you start mixing in his regular food.

If you see that your Beagle starts vomiting again in between treatment, it's best to go and see the veterinarian.

Photo Credit: Heather and Robert Lindberg of Windstar Beagles.

The following symptoms require immediate treatment. Call a veterinarian right away.

1. Your dog's vomit is bright green in color. Green dye is usually found in some types of rodenticides (poisons) meant to kill rats and mice.

2. Your dog's vomit has red blood or ground coffee-like material. Both can be signs of gastrointestinal bleeding.

3. Your dog has shown repeated attempts at vomiting with each attempt producing nothing. It's a symptom of a potentially dangerous condition known as volvulus and gastric dilatation.

4. There is pain in or enlargement of the dog's abdomen.

5. Urination is decreased. This can occur with signs of dehydration.

6. If your Beagle is vomiting severely and has severe diarrhea, it can lead to dehydration.

7. Your Beagle becomes lethargic and depressed, which shows how his body is seriously affected.

8. Your dog has projectile vomiting, which can be a sign of an obstructed gastrointestinal tract.

9. Your dog vomits frequently, which can make him debilitated. This is usually seen among puppies and older dogs.

Vomiting and Its Diagnosis

It is advised that cases of repetitive, prolonged, and severe vomiting need to be placed under a thorough investigation.

Veterinarians are highly capable of reaching a diagnosis on the underlying condition behind your dog's vomiting by doing certain procedures. These include getting information on the health history and lifestyle of your dog, conducting a physical examination, and potentially running several tests such as biopsies, ultrasound imaging, urinalysis, fecal analysis, blood test, X-rays, and other diagnostic tests. You can also bring a sample of your dog's stool and vomit, which may help in the diagnostic process.

What You Can Do to Prevent Vomiting

While it is true that several causes of vomiting among dogs have no ways of prevention, there are some things you can do to help:

1. Remember to keep an eye on an overly-inquisitive dog, particularly when you are out and about. You may want to keep a basket muzzle handy to make sure that your dog doesn't eat anything that is non-edible.

2. Make sure that your Beagle does not scavenge. Scavenging is said to be the root cause of gastroenteritis. It's also believed to be capable of increasing the risk of toxin exposure and ingestion of foreign bodies.

3. Never allow your dog to consume table scraps. This is because there are some human foods which have dangerous content and therefore should never be fed to dogs. Some types of food that are not "dog-friendly" include macadamia nuts, garlic, onions, chocolate, and grapes.

4. Never give bones to your dog that can break into sharp shards. Otherwise, you can allow the large bone types such as the knuckles or femurs so long as they are uncooked.

5. Make sure that your dog's toys are safe and not a choking hazard.

6. Avoid a sudden change in your Beagle's diet. If you need to make changes, do it gradually. Sudden changes in your dog's dietary habit have been attributed to be the common cause of intestinal upset.

Bloat

Any dog can suffer from bloat. The condition is the second-most common cause of death in dogs, behind cancer.

Some breeds are at higher risk than others. Also known as gastric dilation/volvulus or GDV, bloat cannot be treated with an antibiotic or prevented with a vaccine. In roughly 50% of cases, bloat is fatal.

In severe cases, the stomach twists partially or completely. This causes circulation problems throughout the digestive system. Dogs that do not receive treatment go into cardiac arrest. Even if surgical intervention is attempted, there is no guarantee of success.

Signs of bloat are often mistaken for indications of excess gas. The dog may salivate and attempt to vomit, pace, and whine. Gas reduction products at this stage can be helpful. As the stomach swells, it places pressure on surrounding vital organs, and may burst. All cases of bloat are a serious medical emergency.

Larger dogs with deep chests and small waists face a greater risk of developing bloat. These include the Great Dane, Weimaraner, Saint Bernard, Irish Setter, and the Standard Poodle. Despite being a smaller-sized dog, the Beagle is unfortunately also at risk.

Eating habits also factor into the equation. Dogs that eat one large meal per day consisting of dry food are in a high-risk category. Feed three small meals throughout the day instead. This helps to prevent gulping, which leads to ingesting large amounts of air.

If your Beagle is on a dry food diet, don't let him drink lots of water after eating. Doing so causes the dry food in the stomach to expand, leading to discomfort, and a dilution of the digestive juices.

Limit the amount of play and exercise after meals. A slow walk promotes digestion, but a vigorous romp can be dangerous.

Stress also contributes to bloat, especially in anxious or nervous dogs. Changes in routine, confrontations with other dogs, and moving to a new home can all trigger an attack.

Dogs between the ages of four and seven are at an increased risk. Bloat occurs most often between 2 a.m. and 6 a.m., roughly 10 hours after the animal has had his dinner.

Test your dog's dry food by putting a serving in a bowl with water. Leave the material to expand overnight. If the degree of added bulk seems excessive, consider switching to a premium or organic food.

Keep an anti-gas medicine with simethicone on hand (consult with your veterinarian on correct dosage). Consider adding a probiotic to your dog's food to reduce gas in the stomach and to improve digestive health.

If a dog experiences bloat once, his risk of a future episode is greater. Keep copies of his medical records at home, and know the location of the nearest emergency vet clinic.

Photo Credit: Samantha Goldberg of Molesend Beagles.

Allergies

Like humans, dogs suffer from allergies. Allergies can come from a number of sources, not just pollen. Food, airborne particles, and materials that touch the skin can all cause negative reactions.

Sam Goldberg of BeagleHealth.info: "One of the commonest causes of allergies in dogs is house dust mites, and it is a good idea to suggest having the dog tested for causes so that the vet can advise on ways to control allergies."

Owners tend to notice changes in behavior that suggest discomfort like itching. **Common symptoms** include chewing or biting of the tail, stomach, or hind legs, or licking of the paws.

In reaction to inhaled substances, the dog will sneeze, cough, or experience watering eyes. Ingested substances may lead to vomiting or diarrhea. Dogs can also suffer from rashes or a case of hives. Your poor Beagle can be just as miserable as you are during an allergy attack.

If the reaction occurs in the spring or fall, the likely culprit is **seasonal pollen** or, in the case of hot weather, **fleas**.

If your dog is allergic to something inside your home, he'll have year-round symptoms.

If he's reacting is to something outdoors, it could very well be a seasonal problem and in this case **foot soaks** are good to do because chances are that the allergen is coming inside on their feet, and this stops it spreading round the house.

Consider investing in an **air purifier** to control dust mites and ensure all cleaning products are non-toxic — these could also be the cause of the allergy. Vacuum and change bedding more frequently.

Flea allergy dermatitis (FAD) is a very common condition affecting dogs. It is not the bite of the flea that causes most of the itching, it's the reaction to the saliva.

Consider whether your Beagle is over-vaccinated or over-medicated, as these can affect your pet's immune system and set the stage for allergic conditions. The right balance of gut bacteria is crucial for health, and there is evidence that antibiotics can wipe out good bacteria (as well as the bad).

Your vet may recommend bathing the dog in cool, soothing water, which not only feels pleasurable but washes away the allergens. Special diets are also extremely helpful. Relieving symptoms without addressing the source of the problem is a short-term fix to what can become a lifelong health problem. Usually the more your Beagle gets exposure to an irritant, the more his sensitivity and reaction increases.

For acne-like chin rashes, switch to stainless steel, glass, or ceramic food dishes. Plastic feeding dishes cause this rash, which looks like blackheads surrounded by inflamed skin. Wash the dog's face in clear, cool water and ask the vet for an antibiotic cream to speed the healing process.

General Signs of Illness

Any of the following symptoms can point to a serious medical problem. Have your pet evaluated for any of these behaviors. Don't wait out of fear that you are just being an alarmist. Vets can resolve most medical problems in dogs if treatment starts at the first sign of illness.

Coughing and/or Wheezing

Occasional coughing is not a cause for concern, but if it goes on for more than a week, a vet visit is in order. A cough may indicate:

- kennel cough
- heartworm
- cardiac disease
- bacterial infections
- parasites
- tumors
- allergies

The upper respiratory condition called 'Kennel Cough Syndrome' presents with dry hacking. It is a form of canine bronchitis caused by warm, overcrowded conditions with poor ventilation. In most cases, kennel cough resolves on its own, but do take it seriously, as it can lead to fatal bronchopneumonia in an older dog and in dogs with an underlying heart condition can lead to heart failure.

Infections can last up to 6 weeks. Your Beagle should be kept isolated until several days after they stop coughing. Any dog that has come into contact with an affected dog should also be isolated, as they may transmit the kennel cough to other dogs. Consult with your veterinarian. The doctor may prescribe a cough suppressant or suggest the use of a humidifier to soothe your pet's irritated airways.

When the cause of a cough is unclear, the vet will take a full medical history and order tests, including blood work and X-rays. Fluid may also be drawn from the lungs for analysis. Among other conditions, the doctor will be attempting to rule out heartworms.

If your dog has a heart murmur, they may cough. Get a chest X-ray to see if the heart is enlarged.

Dental Care

Chewing is a dog's only means of maintaining his teeth. Many of our canine friends develop dental problems early in life because they don't get enough of this activity. Not all dogs are prone to cavities.

Most do suffer from accumulations of plaque and associated gum diseases. Often, severe halitosis (bad breath) is the first sign that something is wrong.

With dental problems, gingivitis develops first and, if unaddressed, progresses to periodontitis. Warning signs of gum disease include:

- a reluctance to finish meals
- extreme bad breath
- swollen and bleeding gums
- irregular gum line
- plaque build-up
- drooling and/or loose teeth

Beagles are prone to developing gum and tooth disease because their jaws tend to be small and often their teeth are crowded. The bacterial gum infection periodontitis causes inflammation, gum recession, and possible tooth loss. It requires treatment with antibiotics to prevent a spread of the infection to other parts of the body. Symptoms include:

- pus at the gum line
- loss of appetite
- depression
- irritability
- pawing at the mouth
- trouble chewing
- loose or missing teeth

- gastrointestinal upset

Treatment begins with a professional cleaning. This procedure may also involve root work, descaling, and even extractions.

With Proliferating Gum Disease, the gums overgrow the teeth, causing inflammation and infection. Other symptoms include:

- thickening and lengthening of the gums
- bleeding
- bad breath
- drooling
- loss of appetite

The vet will prescribe antibiotics, and surgery is usually required.

Diabetes

Canines can suffer from three types of diabetes: insipidus, diabetes mellitus, and gestational diabetes. All point to malfunctioning endocrine glands and are often linked to poor diet. Larger dogs are in a higher risk category.

- In cases of **diabetes insipidus**, low levels of the hormone vasopressin create problems with the regulation of blood glucose, salt, and water.

- **Diabetes mellitus** is more common and dangerous. It is divided into Types I and II. The first develops in young dogs and may be referred to as "juvenile." Type II is more prevalent in adult and older dogs. All cases are treated with insulin.

- **Gestational diabetes** occurs in pregnant female dogs and requires the same treatment as diabetes mellitus. Obese dogs are at greater risk.

Abnormal insulin levels interfere with blood sugar levels. Any dog that is obese is at a higher risk for developing diabetes.

Symptoms of Canine Diabetes

All of the following behaviors are signs that a dog is suffering from canine diabetes:

- excessive water consumption
- excessive and frequent urination
- weight gain (or loss) for no apparent reason
- lethargy/uncharacteristic laziness

It is possible your Beagle may display no symptoms whatsoever. Diabetes can be slow to develop, so the effects may not be immediately noticeable. Regular check-ups help to catch this disease, which can be fatal even when you do not realize that anything is wrong.

Managing Diabetes

As part of a diabetes management program, the vet will recommend diet changes, including special food. Your dog may need insulin injections. Although this may sound daunting, your vet will train you to administer the shots.

A dog with diabetes can live a full and normal life. Expect regular visits to the vet to check for heart and circulatory problems.

Canine Eye Care

Check your dog's eyes on a regular schedule to avoid problems like clogged tear ducts. Also, many dogs suffer from excessive tearing, which can stain the fur around the eyes and down the muzzle.

As a part of good grooming, keep the corners of your pet's eyes and the muzzle free of mucus to prevent bacterial growth. If your dog is prone to mucus accumulation, ask your vet for sterile eyewash or gauze pads. Also consider having the dog tested for environmental allergies.

With longhaired animals, take the precaution of keeping the hair well-trimmed around your pet's eyes. If you do not feel comfortable doing this chore yourself, discuss the problem with your groomer. Shorter hair prevents the transference of bacteria and avoids trauma from scrapes and scratches.

Dogs love to hang their heads out of car windows, but this can result in eye injuries and serious infection from blowing debris. There is a product called Doggles, which are protective goggles for dogs in a range of colors and sizes for less than $20 / £12 per pair, but I would really **advise against** allowing your dog to let it stick its head out the window in the first place, as it is a dangerous habit.

Conjunctivitis

Conjunctivitis, otherwise known as *pink eye*, is the most common eye infection seen in dogs. It presents with redness around the eyes and a green or yellow discharge. Antibiotics will treat the infection. The dreaded "cone of shame" collar then prevents more injury from scratching during healing.

What are the various types and symptoms of conjunctivitis?

1. The conjunctiva is described as the moist tissue that acts like a covering of the frontal area of the eyeball, as well as a lining around the eyelids. Conjunctivitis occurs when there is redness in the eye's moist tissues.

2. There is the unusual habit of squinting or spasmodic blinking.

3. Your dog's eyes produce a discharge, which is either clear or has mucus/pus content.

4. There is swelling as a result of the build-up of fluid in the eye's moist tissues.

5. Follicle formation gives the moist tissue area of the eyelids a cobblestone appearance. Follicles are actually accumulation of lymphoid tissues that are said to have lymphocytes.

What causes conjunctivitis?

Conjunctivitis may be caused by several factors that range from viral, bacterial, to cancer and more. Viral causes of conjunctivitis have been solely attributed to the so-called **canine distemper** virus.

Bacterial causes can classify conjunctivitis as either a primary condition or neonatal. The latter involves newborn inflammation around the moist tissues in the eye area caused by accumulation of discharge. The discharge is usually seen before the dog's eyelids open or before they separate.

At times, conjunctivitis has also been linked to signs of cancer. Some of these signs include tumors (rare); lesions; inflammation of the border that is found between the cornea and the sclera; and presence of nodules that appear like a pink mass.

Conjunctivitis can also be a secondary condition brought by various diseases and environmental causes. These include lash diseases; lid diseases; lack of normal tear film or dry eye; irritation from eye medications, chemicals or dust; foreign body in the eye's moist tissues; glaucoma; anterior uveitis; and ulcerative keratitis.

Conjunctivitis and its diagnosis

In getting a diagnosis, the veterinarian would first look for evidence of other eye diseases. This is to find out whether conjunctivitis is also evident in other parts of the eye apart from the conjunctiva. An eye exam is usually conducted wherein various methods of examination are used.

One method uses the so-called "fluorescein stain," wherein the surface of the eye is spread with fluorescein. This allows ulcers, scratches, and foreign material to appear more visible under the light. This type of method is an ideal way to rule out ulcerative keratitis. The dog's lids or eyelashes are also examined thoroughly to check for the presence of foreign materials.

Pressures in the eye are also determined in order to diagnose glaucoma while the nasal cavity is sometimes flushed out to diagnose the presence of disease in the area.

If the eye brings out a discharge, the vet will perform a culture in order to determine the components of the discharge, which can indicate an infection. Microscopic examination may also be conducted by collecting a biopsy of conjunctiva cells.

Lastly, the vet may run a skin test if there is a reason to suspect skin allergies as the underlying cause of conjunctivitis.

Cataracts

A cataract is clouding or darkening in the lens of the eye that results from accumulated proteins leading to blurred vision.

Surgery is the only permanent solution for this problem, though many Beagles adapt well to changes in vision — even total loss of vision. You should have your dog's cataracts checked by a veterinarian in any case, however, to rule out secondary complications.

In most cases, the vet will watch, but not treat, cataracts. The condition does not affect your pet's life in a severe way. Dogs adapt well to the senses they do have, so diminished vision is not as problematic as it would be for us.

Glaucoma

Glaucoma in dogs is a health condition characterized by pressure that is placed on the eye, which causes the latter to suffer from inadequate fluid drainage. When the condition reaches a chronic state or it continues without any treatment, the dog can experience blindness as a result of the permanent damage to his optic nerve.

The bad news is that 40 percent of affected dogs will experience blindness in the affected eye within just the first year of being diagnosed with the condition. This is particularly true whether the dog received medical or surgical treatment.

What are the types and symptoms of glaucoma in dogs?

Glaucoma in dogs has two main types: primary and secondary. Primary open angle glaucoma Beagle type (POAG) is an eye disorder causing a build-up of pressure in the eye.

Symptoms of sudden occurrence of glaucoma include:

1. Loss of vision
2. Dilated pupil or the pupil being unresponsive to light
3. Cloudy appearance at the eye's front part
4. Unnatural blinking of the eye
5. Blood vessels in the eye's whites appearing obviously red
6. Receding eyeball back into the dog's head
7. High pressure felt within the eye

Glaucoma, in the long term, is said to develop into certain advanced diseases. These include advanced degeneration within the dog's eye, obvious vision loss, and *bupthalmos*, or enlargement of the eyeball.

Secondary glaucoma in dogs is more common compared to primary glaucoma and is said to be caused by secondary eye infections. Symptoms include the following:

1. Suspected circular sticking of the iris' edge to the lens
2. Suspected sticking of the iris either to the lens or to the cornea
3. Suspected pupil constriction
4. Inflammatory debris in the front part of the eye
5. Cloudy appearance at the front part of the eye
6. Unusual redness of the blood vessels in the eyes' whites
7. High pressure found within the eye

Other notable symptoms of glaucoma include less desire to interact or play; obvious change in attitude; absence of appetite; and headaches.

Glaucoma and its diagnosis

In order to have an accurate diagnosis, you should be able to provide a comprehensive health history of your dog. This will include symptoms that have occurred as far as you can remember and notable incidents that could have contributed to the condition. One example would be injuries to the eye regardless whether they are minor or major.

When conducting a physical examination, the vet will use a tonometer on the eye's surface in order to test the pressure within. If glaucoma has been diagnosed as a sudden disease, the vet will advise you to take your dog to a veterinary ophthalmologist. The latter will conduct detailed examination on both eyes. This includes using gonioscopy, which is the method of measuring the eye's anterior in order to evaluate its filtration angles.

They will also perform the so-called **electroretinography** for the purpose of determining whether the eye will remain blind even after treatment. On the other hand, abnormalities in the eye are usually detected through ultrasound and X-rays in secondary diseases.

When the dog has been diagnosed to have glaucoma in one eye, certain measures are taken to protect and prevent the unaffected eye from suffering the same condition.

Cherry Eye

Dogs have a unique anatomy of their eyes. They have up to 6 eyelids, with each eye having 3. These are the upper eyelid, the lower lid, and the third eyelid, which we seldom see. Otherwise known as nictitating membranes, the dog's third eyelids normally lie beneath the lower lids.

Both the upper and lower eyelids function very much like human eyelids. The third eyelids act like an extra layer of eye protection in dogs. It's like a wipe that helps in keeping the eye clear of dust and debris. It also has a tear gland that increases moisture in the dog's eye by around 35 percent.

The dog's third eyelids also have glands that are found in the corner of the eye right next to his nose. Sometimes the gland slips out of place and appears like it is bulging. This bulge, which is similar to a red or pinkish blob, is what's known as *cherry eye*.

Although the exact causes of cherry eye are not well understood, there are certain things about it that we should be aware of.

1. Cherry eye is neither a true medical emergency nor a life-threatening condition. Dogs with cherry eye feel a number of discomforts. This includes inflammation, irritation, eye redness (conjunctivitis), and others. To relieve the discomfort, dogs should be treated promptly at the veterinarian clinic. The move will also help in preventing permanent ocular damage.

2. It is possible that the cherry eye condition will correct by itself in a couple of weeks. However, waiting for this to happen can be frustrating. The longer time that the gland is out of place, the bigger it becomes due to swelling. Since it is bigger, it is harder to reposition it. Moreover, there's a huge chance that the condition will occur again. If left untreated, it can later lead to a more serious problem.

3. Dogs that are younger, around 6 weeks to 2 years, are more likely to be seen with a cherry eye. While any breed can develop the condition, cherry eye is more commonly found in Neapolitan Mastiffs, Miniature Poodles, Lhasa Apsos, Pekingese, Beagles, Shih Tzus, Shar-Peis, Cocker Spaniels, Bulldogs, Bloodhounds, Newfoundlands, and Boston Terriers.

Ruth Darlene Stewart of Aladar Beagles: "I personally have seen some as early as 8 weeks and as late as 10 years of age. Treatment may

Photo Credit: Ruth Darlene Stewart of Aladar Beagles.

consist of simple application of an appropriate ophthalmic ointment and reduction of the prolapse by your veterinarian.

"I have seen only one cherry eye stay in, once placed back in its proper position and treated with ointment only (to reduce the swelling). Typically they will pop back out and then you must surgically treat them. Since

30% of the dog's tear production can come from the involved gland you must discuss each option with your veterinarian carefully. DRY EYE or Keratoconjunctivitis Sicca (KCS) can result from its removal. Since Beagles are prone to develop DRY EYE, this is a major reason to not surgically remove the gland, although this is a method used widely in the U.S."

The two methods for surgical treatment are:

1. TACKING — a properly trained veterinarian surgically sutures the gland back into its normal position. The tear production is not altered with this method. There is chance that the cherry eye will pop back out. Some resources have it at 10–30% reoccurrence rate.

2. REMOVAL — this method is quick and usually a cautery procedure is used. The gland is removed.

Sam Goldberg of BeagleHealth.info: "Cherry eye can be traumatic, and I have known Beagles who have had a bang to the face or rough play where a cherry eye has appeared, been replaced, and not come back out. The eye specialist we use in our practice says that in practice few dogs develop dry eye (or they would have had it anyway) so removal, which is less traumatic than replacement, is generally fine."

Canine Arthritis

Dogs, like humans, can suffer from arthritis, which may develop in the presence of hip or elbow dysplasia as a secondary complication. Arthritis is a debilitating degeneration of the joints and is common in larger breeds. As the cartilage in the joints breaks down, the action of bone rubbing on bone creates considerable pain. In turn, the animal's range of motion becomes restricted.

Standard treatments do not differ from those used for humans. Aspirin addresses pain and inflammation, while supplements like glucosamine work on improving joint health. Environmental aids, like steps and ramps, ease the strain on the affected joints and help pets stay active.

Arthritis also occurs as a natural consequence of aging. Management focuses on making your pet comfortable and facilitating ease of motion. Some dogs become so crippled that their humans buy mobility carts for them.

Hip and Elbow Dysplasia

Any breed can be susceptible to hip dysplasia. This defect prevents the leg bones from fitting properly into the hip joint. It is a painful condition that causes limping in the hindquarters. The condition may be inherited, or the consequence of injury and aging.

The standard treatment is anti-inflammatory medication. Some cases need surgery and even a full joint replacement. Surgical intervention for this defect carries a high success rate, allowing your dog to live a full and happy life.

Luxating Patella

A dog with a luxating patella experiences frequent dislocations of the kneecap. The condition is common in smaller breeds, and can affect one or both kneecaps. Surgery may be required to rectify the problem.

Often, owners have no idea anything is wrong with their dog's knee joint. Then the pet jumps off a bed or leaps to catch a toy, lands badly, and begins to limp and favor the other leg.

The condition may be genetic in origin, so it is important to ask a breeder if the problem has surfaced in the line of dogs he cultivates.

A luxating patella can also be the consequence of a physical injury, especially as a dog ages. For this reason, you want to discourage jumping in older dogs. Offer steps in key locations around the home to help your senior Beagle navigate in safety.

Any time you see your dog limping or seeming more fatigued than usual after vigorous play, have the dog checked out. Conditions like a luxating patella only get worse with time and wear, and need immediate treatment.

Classic signs are skipping as the patella luxates as they flex the stifle — this is the knee joint between the thigh bone (the femur) and the two lower leg bones (tibia and fibula).

Beagle Tail

This usually occurs after bathing or swimming when a Beagle has shaken itself to dry off. You notice the top half of his tail seemingly numb and limp. It is a worry because he appears to be in pain and it is not silly to imagine his tail is broken. Usually with a few days rest or anti-inflammatory medication, the tail returns to normal and it may never occur again.

The Matter of Genetic Abnormalities

Although responsible breeders work hard to eliminate potential genetic illnesses from their blood lines, there are some conditions for which there are no screening tests available.

Also, Beagles that come from backyard breeders do not benefit from the same genetic cultivation and are even more susceptible to health issues. Before you adopt a Beagle, you should be aware of the possibility of the following conditions, all of which are associated with the breed.

Neonatal Cerebellar Cortical Degeneration (NCCD)

This is a degenerative and currently untreatable disease of the cerebellum, the part of the brain involved with movement and motor control of the body. Many people in the U.S. will know it as "Tumbling Puppy Syndrome." As soon as a Beagle puppy starts walking, this will be apparent, and many breeders opt to euthanize them.

Ruth Darlene Stewart of Aladar Beagles explains the symptoms: "A puppy is slower to walk than its littermates. It is very unsteady on its feet and often circles to the same side or falls to the same side. You notice a head tilt and odd side-to-side movement of the eyes. The puppy acts uncoordinated, like a drunk person, it staggers and falls!! Sometimes with maturity the puppy can walk straight, but when trying to move at a fast pace such as a trot, the uncoordinated side motions return. The puppy seems to fall over its own feet and runs to one side. Going up or down stairs is a challenge."

In the U.K., the Animal Health Trust offer a DNA test for this recessive gene (they also can test for MLS). The test for this is available from several labs in the U.S. also. Carriers are healthy, but a Beagle will be affected and show the disease if they carry two copies of the mutant gene. If two carriers are bred together, 25% of puppies could carry two copies of the gene and thus be affected with the disease.

http://www.aht.org.uk/cms-display/genetics_tests.html

Beagle Pain Syndrome

Beagle Pain Syndrome is the common name for Steroid Responsive Meningitis. It was first discovered in Beagles in the 1980s, but the condition can occur in other breeds. The exact cause is unknown, but it may be an immune system disorder. The possible symptoms include:

- cervical pain
- a hunched stance
- shaking
- loss of appetite
- fever
- stiffness in the neck
- muscle spasms in the neck and/or legs
- weakness
- jaw pain exhibited by a reluctance to eat, bark, or howl

The degree of pain varies by individual, but may be so severe the dog whimpers at the slightest movement. The condition typically presents at age 4–10 months, but can occur at any time. Definitive diagnosis is based on a spinal tap and/or an MRI scan.

Ruth Darlene Stewart of Aladar Beagles: "Ideally, both tests should be performed. In some cases, testing may not be readily available or affordable to the owners. Some owners and veterinarians have opted to start high dose steroid treatment and see if the dog responds quickly — if so, additional testing is not done.

"Treatment is with steroids, specifically prednisolone or prednisone at dosages between 1–4mg/kg/day. A protocol used by Dr. Samantha Goldberg is to start on 2mg/kg twice daily and after 5–7 days slowly start weaning down. Then maintain the patient on twice weekly 5mg for a few months when they have been badly affected, and this will often hold them until they are older. In more severe cases, other immunosuppressive agents, such as Azathiorpine or Cytarabine, may be used in conjunction with corticosteroid steroid therapy.

"The main goal is to start treatment quickly and with adequate dosages. High steroid treatment should be first-line treatment. Weaning off the medication should be done gradually, as cases have shown that relapses may occur quickly if the steroid therapy is discontinued too rapidly. Do not start weaning until the dog is totally back to normal.

"Steroid treatment will make the dog drink more water and may cause water retention. The side effects of the treatment (excessive eating, drinking, and urinating, including numerous "accidents") can be overwhelming to the average pet owner. Moving can be painful for them, so if the dog lives in an active household with kids and other dogs, confining the dog in a crate or separate area is suggested."

Epilepsy

Beagles have both early onset epilepsy and late onset epilepsy that is common in the breed. It is in every line in North America, and there is no current test to determine carriers of this horrible condition.

Epilepsy is a widely used term describing the uncontrolled movements of muscles known as convulsions, fits, and seizures. These can start from 2–5 years of age and it is possibly stress-related, but we just don't know for sure.

These seizures usually last a minute or two (often during sleep) but can sometimes be repeated over and over (cluster seizures) or be prolonged (status epilepticus). Evidence of urine or feces in their bed could indicate they had a seizure during sleep.

Treatment usually involves the drug phenobarbitone to reduce or remove the seizures.

A DNA test is available for the rare Lafora disease, which is an inherited late onset progressive myoclonic epilepsy.

Pyruvate Kinase Deficiency

Pyruvate Kinase (PK) is an enzyme that plays an important role in energy generation, and its deficiency impairs the red blood cell's ability to metabolize, which in turn may cause anemia and other blood-related issues. Beagles may be weakened and depressed, with a decreased appetite, pale gums, and a lethargic, sleepy demeanor. Both heart rate and respiration will show increases. Diagnosis is based on symptoms, a blood work-up, iron testing, urinalysis, and bone marrow testing.

Bone marrow transplantation is the only available treatment for PK-deficient dogs. However, this treatment is expensive and potentially life-threatening.

Musladine Lueke Syndrome

MLS was formerly known as Chinese Beagle Syndrome due to the slant of the Beagles eyes owing to the tight skin and higher ear set. Affected dogs have short outer toes that cause them to walk on their front legs like a ballerina on point. It is not unusual for all four feet to be affected.

The dog's skin is overly tight and feels hard to the touch, giving the appearance of a well-muscled dog. The Beagle will also carry its tail straight and stiff. Generally the syndrome is evident by 2–4 weeks.

Progression of the disease stabilizes by one year of age. There is a genetic marker test to determine if a Beagle is a carrier of the syndrome available from many genetic labs in the U.S. and U.K.

Even dogs with a perfectly normal appearance can be carriers. Dogs with MLS typically have a perfectly normal lifespan, but clearly they should never be used in a breeding program. There are now many Beagles who are hereditarily clear as both parents are clear.

Bev Davies-Fraser of Waskasoo Kennel and WindyHill Beagles: "I have attached pictures of this condition. Two littermates, side by side. You can see the difference quite easily. Some Vets STILL do not know what the condition is and now it is only being recognized when breeders discuss the condition with them."

Photo Credit: Bev Davies-Fraser of Waskasoo Kennel and WindyHill Beagles.

Photo Credit: Bev Davies-Fraser of Waskasoo Kennel and WindyHill Beagles.

Factor VII Deficiency

This is a bleeding disorder specifically causing clotting issues. Deficiency of Factor VII can lead to mild to moderate bleeding when a Beagle incurs bruising or a minor injury.

Some Beagles can have a blood clotting disorder that causes excessive or prolonged bleeding after an injury or surgery. Either their body doesn't produce enough factor VII, or something is interfering with their factor VII, often another medical condition.

Factor VII is a protein produced in the liver that plays an important role in helping blood to clot and also occurs in humans.

A recessive disorder means that a dog needs to carry two copies of the mutant gene to be affected and have problems. Many affected Beagles do not have severe bleeding problems and can be safely mated to a clear dog without producing affected puppies.

Imerslund-Grasbeck Syndrome

IGS affects the body's ability to absorb Vitamin B12 from the diet, and also occurs in other breeds such as Border Collies, Australian Shepherds, and Giant Schnauzers. Vitamin B12 is important for red blood cell production and the development and maintenance of the nervous system.

IGS can be treated by injections to affected dogs, and although the incidence is low in the U.K., it is quite widely found in some Beagle populations elsewhere. A DNA test is available.

In Beagles it is inherited as a recessive condition, meaning they have to have two copies of the gene to be affected. If two carriers are mated together, then 25% of the puppies born can be affected. If either parent is clear, then the disease is not seen, as puppies can only be carrier or clear.

Affected Beagles can develop macrocytic anemia, and warning signs include low appetite and growth, as well as neurological signs as the nerve structure does not develop correctly.

They require weekly supplementation by injection or they will eventually die. If treated early enough they may recover back to normal.

Chondrodystrophy

This is a type of "dwarfism" caused by abnormal growth in the leg bones and vertebrae of Beagles. They tend to have crooked front legs, a short neck, a large head, a curved back, and an awkward gait.

This genetic condition means that any affected Beagles should not be bred from. The good news is that in a mild form dogs can live long and happy lives, although more severely affected Beagles may have to be euthanized. Signs are usually apparent from about three to four weeks of age, and the condition can be confirmed by X-rays.

Bev Davies-Fraser of Waskasoo Kennel: "There currently isn't any genetic test for this condition, but they have identified some of the markers. A Beagle with chondrodystrophy is often mistaken as a Basset Hound cross. Bassets & Dachshunds are chondrodystrophic breeds by nature and design, where Beagles with this condition occasionally show up in an otherwise perfectly normal litter."

Sam Goldberg of BeagleHealth.info: "The Beagle is considered to be a chondrondystrophic breed by some vets. Certainly the very small ones can be sometimes inadvertently be affected by selection for height."

Hypothyroidism

Hypothyroidism occurs when the thyroid gland fails to produce adequately. The deficiency of the hormone causes:

- obesity
- lack of energy
- dulled mental abilities
- infertility

The dog's hair may change, becoming brittle, dull, and falling out altogether, while the skin gets dark and tough.

The condition can be managed with daily medication that must be continued for life.

Cardiac Disorders

Although rare, heart conditions seen in the breed include:

- dilated cardiomyopathy (typically diagnosed when the dog develops a persistent cough and won't eat)
- pulmonic stenosis (enlargement of the right side of the heart with an accompanying murmur)
- ventricular septal defect (a hole in the heart)

All are managed with medication, but significantly reduce the animal's projected lifespan.

Lymphosarcoma

The third-most diagnosed cancer in dogs, lymphosarcoma is cancer of the lymphocytes and lymphoid tissues present in the lymph nodes, liver, spleen, gastrointestinal tract, and bone marrow. The cancer typically presents at 6–9 years with both genders at equal risk, but the prognosis for neutered females is better. Although there have been tremendous advances in canine oncology, most dogs with some form of lymphoma succumb to the disease in 4–6 weeks after diagnosis.

There is a less frequent type of lymphoma being reported — subcutaneous lymphoma. This type presents as skin lesions or oral lesions.

Pituitary-Dependant Hyperadrenocorticism

Pituitary-dependant Hyperadrenocorticism, or Cushing's Disease, in dogs results in chronic over-production of glucocorticoid by the adrenal glands. It can be caused be a problem in the pituitary gland, which signals the adrenals to produce the hormone, or in the adrenals themselves (when it is referred to as adrenal-based hyperadrenocorticism.)

The condition is a complicated one with a number of symptoms. The most common are:

- increased water consumption and urination
- increased appetite with enlargement of the abdomen
- thinning of the skin with accompanying hair loss

The condition is diagnosed with a range of lab tests beginning with a complete blood work-up, urinalysis, an abdominal ultrasound, and a low-dose dexamethasone suppression test.

About 80% of the cases in dogs are of the pituitary type, which responds to oral doses of various drugs to regulate pituitary function. The disease affects middle age and older dogs and is considered manageable if accurately diagnosed.

Photo Credit: Natasha Bell of Alfadais Beagles.

Intervertebral Disk Disease

Like Dachshunds, Beagles often develop intervertebral disk disease (IVD or IVDD). The condition presents with herniated disks in the lower back that cause severe pain that may radiate up to the neck.

Sam Goldberg of BeagleHealth.info: "IVDD in the neck is one of the commonest differential diagnoses for neck pain in Beagles over 2 years old. It is possibly more common than IVDD in the lower back of the Beagle."

Depending on the extent of the issue, surgery may be required, with some Beagles experiencing rear-quarter paralysis and the need for medical assistance carts to remain mobile.

These devices, which attach to the hips, put your pooch on wheels. Beagles adapt well under such circumstances. So long as your pet is otherwise healthy, this is a reasonable approach to a debilitating, but not fatal ailment.

Often called "dog wheelchairs," you can buy these units online from sites like http://www.handicappedpets.com.

Although the carts are adjustable, having your dog custom fitted for the appliance may provide more mobility.

To help guard against instances of IVD, Beagle owners should not allow their dogs to engage in activities that unduly strain their backs and spines, including excessive jumping or actions that require sudden twisting.

You should also keep your Beagle well-exercised, fed a balanced diet, and at an ideal body condition (not too lean and not overweight). Allow your Beagle to mature fully before considering neutering.

The main warning signs to watch for include pain (arching of the back, yelping unprovoked), incoordination such as stumbling and swaying, and paralysis.

Cage rest (typically over 6–8 weeks) combined with anti-inflammatory medication and painkillers are the main conservative treatment approaches likely to be recommended by your vet, where surgery is not felt to be necessary.

Most dogs that have surgery within 24 hours of becoming paralyzed have more rapid and complete recoveries than dogs that have surgery at a later time. If a dog is paralyzed, but still has deep pain sensations, surgery can often result in a complete recovery or a reasonably good recovery with minor neurological deficits.

Chapter 12 — Helping Your Senior Beagle Live Longer

Obviously it can be incredibly sad to see your beloved Beagle grow older. Unfortunately, aging is a natural part of life that cannot be avoided. All you can do is to learn how to provide for your Beagle's needs as he ages so you can keep him with you for as long as possible.

He may develop health problems like arthritis, and he simply might not be as active as he once was. You are likely to notice a combination of both physical and mental (behavior) changes, as both body and mind start to slow. However, with good veterinary care and proper nutrition, he can live for many more years and you can help extend this.

Sam Goldberg of BeagleHealth.info: "One of the biggest contributors to longevity is not to fall for the big brown eyes that demand food! Sadly, many older Beagles are overweight, which leads to issues with joints, heart, and skin. The excess fat can produce chemicals that speed up joint deterioration. The fittest Beagles live the longest!"

Elderly Beagles and What to Expect

Aging is a natural part of life for both humans and dogs. Sadly, dogs reach the end of their lives sooner than most humans. Once your Beagle reaches the age of 8 years or so, he can be considered a "senior" dog.

At this point, you may need to start feeding him a dog food specially formulated for older dogs. Because their **metabolism slows down**, they will put on weight unless their daily calories are reduced.

Unfortunately, this weight then places extra stress on their joints and organs, making them work harder than before.

In order to properly care for your Beagle as he ages, you might find it helpful to know what to expect as your dog starts to get older:

1. Your Beagle's **joints** may start to give him trouble — check for signs of swelling and stiffness, often due to arthritis, and consult your veterinarian with any problems.

2. Your dog may be **less active** than he was in his youth — he will likely still enjoy walks, but he may not last as long as he once did, and he might take it at a slower pace.

3. Organs, such as heart or liver, may not function as effectively.

4. He may have an occasional "accident" inside the house as a result of incontinence. He may also urinate more frequently.

5. Your Beagle may **sleep more** than he once did — this is a natural sign of aging, but it can also be a symptom of a health problem, so consult your vet if his sleeping becomes excessive.

6. He may have a greater tendency to **gain weight**, so you will need to carefully monitor his diet to keep him from becoming obese in his old age.

7. Brain activity is affected — your Beagle's **memory**, ability to learn, and awareness will all start to weaken. He may wander round aimlessly or fail to respond to basic commands.

8. He may have **trouble walking** or jumping, so keep an eye on your Beagle if he has difficulty jumping, or if he starts dragging his back feet.

9. You may need to trim your Beagle's nails more frequently if he doesn't spend as much time outside as he once did when he was younger.

10. Your Beagle will develop gray hair around the face and muzzle — this may be less noticeable in Beagles with a lighter coat.

11. Your Beagle's **vision** may deteriorate. Be careful if his eyes appear cloudy. This could be a sign of cataracts, and you should see your vet as soon as you notice this.

12. He may develop halitosis (bad breath), which can be a sign of dental or gum disease. Get this checked out by a vet.

13. He may also become more protective of you around strangers, be increasingly irritable, and bark and whine more.

While many of the signs mentioned above are natural side effects of aging, they can also be symptoms of serious health conditions. If your Beagle develops any of these problems suddenly, consult your veterinarian immediately.

Tips for Caring for Beagles in Old Age

When your Beagle gets older, he may require different care than he did when he was younger. The more you know about what to expect as your Beagle ages, the better equipped you will be to provide him with the care he needs to remain healthy and mobile.

1. Supplement your dog's diet with DHA and EPA fatty acids to help prevent joint stiffness and arthritis.

2. Schedule routine annual visits with your veterinarian to make sure your Beagle is in good condition.

3. Consider switching to a dog food that is specially formulated for senior/mature dogs — a food that is too high in calories may cause your dog to gain weight. Some are labeled as from age 8, others for even older dogs such as 10+. Take it **slow** when switching to minimize the impact on their digestive system, which cannot cope with sudden change.

4. Brush his teeth regularly to prevent periodontal diseases, which are fairly common in older dogs. A daily dental stick helps reduce tartar, freshen breath, and improve gum health.

5. Continue to exercise your Beagle on a regular basis — he may not be able to move as quickly, but you still need to keep him active to maintain joints, muscle health, and vital organs such as heart, lungs, and joints.

6. Provide your Beagle with **soft bedding** on which to sleep — the hard floor may aggravate his joints and worsen arthritis.

7. Ensure his usual environment is not too noisy, as he will need to rest and sleep more to recharge his body. Make sure it is neither too hot nor cold, as his body **may not regulate** his temperature as well as he used to.

8. Put down carpet or rugs on hard floors — slippery hardwood or tile flooring can be very problematic for arthritic dogs.

9. Keep your Beagle's **mind exercised** as well as his body. Playing games and introducing new toys will achieve this.

10. Use **ramps** to get your dog into the car and onto the bed (if he is allowed), because he may no longer be able to jump.

11. Avoid **sugar and grains** which can be acid-forming and pro-inflammatory, as well as being an unnatural food for dogs.

12. Cat's claw is a Peruvian vine that has anti-inflammatory properties and is used for relief from arthritic pain.

13. For rebuilding muscles, skin, cartilage, tendons and ligaments, a good dietary source of vitamin C is necessary, together with an organic form of sulphur (it is a component of collagen).

14. Homoeopathic remedies can help with pain and inflammation too — Arnica can reduce bruising of tissues.

The most important thing you can do for your senior dog is to schedule regular visits with your veterinarian. You should also, however, keep an eye out for signs of disease as your dog ages. If you notice your elderly Beagle exhibiting any of these symptoms, you would be wise to seek veterinary care for your dog as soon as possible:

• Decreased appetite
• Increased thirst and urination
• Difficulty urinating/constipation
• Blood in the urine
• Difficulty breathing/coughing
• Vomiting or diarrhea
• Poor coat condition

Why I Recommend Pet Insurance

I believe in preventive maintenance as much as possible. My own dogs are seen by a veterinary chiropractor fairly regularly from the time they are about 9 weeks old, and they are well-exercised to avoid the "weekend athlete" injuries. I have been blessed with overall sound and healthy Beagles, but nevertheless I wouldn't be without my pet health insurance just in case the worst happens.

Thanks to advances in veterinary science, our pets now receive viable and effective treatments. The estimated annual cost for a medium-sized dog, including healthcare, is $650 / £400 (this does not include emergency care, advanced procedures, or consultations with specialists.) The growing interest in pet insurance to help defray these costs is understandable. You can buy a policy covering accidents, illness, and hereditary and chronic conditions for $25 / £16.25 per month. Benefit caps and deductibles vary by company.

Although breeders are striving to improve the overall health of the Beagle, it is inevitable that you will need to make a number of visits to the vet's in your Beagle's lifetime. Apart from the routine of annual injections and check-ups, there are bound to be unexpected visits, often at weekends or in the middle of the night, when costs are significantly higher. This total can run to thousands of dollars (or pounds).

Establishing a healthy record from the very beginning ensures your Beagle qualifies for full insurance coverage and lower premiums. To get rate quotes, investigate the following companies:

United States

http://www.24PetWatch.com
http://www.ASPCAPetInsurance.com
http://www.PetsBest.com
http://www.PetInsurance.com

United Kingdom

http://www.Animalfriends.org.uk
http://www.Healthy-pets.co.uk
http://www.Petplan.co.uk

Sam Goldberg of BeagleHealth.info: "A good policy should have lifetime coverage, not 12 months only, and checking the level of coverage is worthwhile in the small print, as you really do get what you pay for.

"It is essential to make sure you can look after your Beagle both in the home and at the vet's. It is very frustrating for a vet to know the owner cares and would like to do everything possible, but the finances are not available. Make sure you either insure your dog well or have a savings pot available for any unexpected expenses. Visits to referral specialists can allow many amazing things to be done, but expect to pay a few thousand pounds for the privilege of such up-to-date care. Beagles can live well into their teens, but this means senior costs such as arthritis medication, so make sure you can provide everything you would like to keep your old friend happy."

Grieving a Lost Pet

The hardest decision any pet owner makes is helping a suffering animal to pass easily and humanely. I have been in this position. Even though I know my beloved companions died peacefully and with no pain, my own anguish was considerable. Thankfully, I was in the care of and accepting the advice and counsel of exceptional veterinary professionals.

This is the crucial component in the decision to euthanize an animal. For your own peace of mind, you must know that you have the best medical advice possible. My vet was not only knowledgeable and patient, but she was kind and forthright. I valued those qualities and hope you are as blessed as I was in the same situation.

The bottom line is that you must make the best decision that you can for your pet, and for yourself. So long as you are acting from a position of love, respect, and responsibility, whatever you do is "right."

Photo Credit: Bev Davies-Fraser - this is Rhett who passed at age 13 ½.

Some humans have difficulty fully recognizing the terrible grief involved in losing a beloved canine friend. There will be many who **do not understand** the close bond we humans can have with our dogs, which is often unlike any we have with our human counterparts.

Your friends may give you pitying looks and try to cheer you up, but if they have never experienced the loss of such a special connection themselves, they may also secretly think you are making too much fuss over "just a dog." For some of us humans, the loss of a beloved dog is so painful that we decide never to share our lives with another, because the thought of going through the pain of such a loss is unbearable.

Expect to feel terribly sad, tearful, and yes, depressed, because those who are close to their canine companions will feel their loss no less acutely than the loss of a human friend or life partner. The grieving process can take some time to recover from, and some of us never totally recover.

After the loss of a family dog, first you need to take care of yourself by making certain that you remember to eat regular meals and get enough sleep, even though you will feel an almost eerie sense of loneliness.

Losing a beloved dog is a shock to the system that can also affect your concentration and your ability to find joy or be interested in participating in other activities that are a normal part of your daily life.

Other dogs, cats, and pets in the home will also be grieving the loss of a companion and may display this by acting depressed, being off their food, or showing little interest in play or games. Therefore, you need to help guide your other pets through this grieving process by keeping them busy and interested, taking them for extra walks, and finding ways to spend more time with them.

Bev Davies-Fraser of Waskasoo Kennel: "It is heartbreaking for any Beagle owner to know if it is time to say goodbye to our beloved pet and how to know when the time is right. Many people think that their dog will 'let them know' when the time has come. I came to believe that we owe our Beagles the best life that we can provide for them. When they have been a part of your life for 12–15 years, you can see when things change drastically enough to make the difficult decision. I started a calendar with my boy when it was obvious time was running out. Every day I would make a notation. Good day/bad day. When the bad days outweighed the good days, I made the decision to let my dog pass. A wise person once told me, 'Better a day too soon, than a day too late.' Our pets rely on us to make that decision for them. Make sure you have a vet that is sensitive to your feelings and will provide you with the time to spend with your dog to say goodbye. Euthanasia is the last kind gift we can give to that special dog."

Wait Long Enough

Many people **do not wait long enough** before attempting to replace a lost pet and will immediately go to the local shelter and rescue a deserving dog. While this may help to distract you from your grieving process, this is not really fair to the new fur member of your family.

Bringing a new pet into a home that is depressed and grieving the loss of a long-time canine member may create behavioral problems for the new dog that will be faced with learning all about their new home, while also dealing with the unstable energy of the grieving family.

A better scenario would be to **allow yourself the time to properly grieve** by waiting a minimum of one month to give yourself and your family time to feel happier and more stable before deciding upon sharing your home with another dog.

Afterword

The Beagle is the fifth-most popular companion breed in the United States and is much beloved around the world. He is not, however, a dog without his challenges. This is a highly active breed with both a physical and emotional need for exercise and intellectually engaging activities.

Depending on your own lifestyle and habits, you may have just read about the breed and come away feeling that a Beagle sounds like the most fun imaginable, or a total pain in the backside. Go with your gut. If you have the uneasy feeling that a Beagle is just going to be too much for you, don't be won over by his good looks and bright personality.

If you cannot give this breed time, attention, and a high level of activity, it is not fair to the Beagle to make him a member of your family. Bored Beagles act out, make a lot of racket, and get fat in a hurry.

At their best, however, Beagles can be great family dogs, keeping up easily with even the most rambunctious children. They do wonderfully well with other dogs, and can get on well with cats, especially if they're raised together.

While people do keep Beagles in apartments, it's an iffy proposition at best given the breed's activity level and full-voiced ability to bark, howl, and bay to make sure you know what they're thinking, hearing, seeing, and smelling. This is a great tendency if you want a watch dog, but a bad trait if you're trying to avoid eviction!

The bottom line in any purchase is to consider the needs of the animal first and then to evaluate the fit with your lifestyle. If his life won't work with yours, admire him from afar, as nothing else is fair to a dog of the Beagle's unmistakable and unique quality.

If, however, the Beagle is the right dog for you, he's an affectionate, loyal, smart little hound with a unique take on the world and you can't beat owning this incredible dog.

Phyllis Wright of MPW adds: "Beagles make a wonderful playful pet to own. They are loyal to the one that feeds them, friends to everyone else. They tend to roam if not on leash, and we always tell people to have a fenced yard. Even when Beagles are well-trained, if a squirrel or rodent passes within eyesight they will chase it. The fenced yard also prevents other dogs from going in and your pet is a safer pet. Beagles make a wonderful pet; whether you are young or old, they adapt very well and are happy just being with someone who loves them."

Bev Davies-Fraser of Waskasoo Kennel: "Beagle owners need to have a sense of humor, love an active lifestyle, and enjoy the incredible intelligence of the breed. While Beagles are very easy to train, they make decisions and will do the work on their own terms. This is sometimes challenging, but always fun!! Beagles love their family, especially the kids. If you want a Beagle that will run, fetch, and basically play with you until YOU are tired, then this is the dog for you. They keep their puppy attitude well into their later years. Those eyes, those ears … who can resist?"

SURPRISE – FREE BONUS BOOK!

I wanted to say thank you for purchasing this book and give you a special surprise.

To show my appreciation I have compiled extra material that we just didn't have space for in this book, into a free e-book that you can download.

This gives you even more value by giving you free access to some exclusive bonus interviews with our expert Beagle breeders.

It contains more of an insight into some of the breeders who were actively involved in the making of this book. You will find some cute and funny stories about our loveable Beagles as well as more tips and advice from our breeders.

I would also really appreciate if you could leave a positive review on the website where you bought this book. The more excellent 5-star reviews the book receives, the higher it will appear in the charts. We would really love to get this book to as many Beagle owners as possible.

If you have any comments to help us improve the book, then I would love to hear them personally and we can then revise the book as necessary. This is far more constructive than leaving a harmful negative review.

Thank you once again – to get the free book, just go to the webpage below and follow the instructions. If you have any issues or feedback/comments, please send an email to sales@dogexperts.info

GET THE FREE BONUS INTERVIEWS...

Go to this page on our website to download your free bonus book gift:

https://www.dogexperts.info/beagle/gift/

Relevant Websites

National Beagle Club of America, Inc.
https://www.nationalbeagleclub.org/

The Beagle Club
http://www.thebeagleclub.org

The Beagle Association
http://beagleassociation.org.uk

Beagle Field Trials - AKC
http://www.akc.org/events/field-trials/beagles/

The Kennel Club - U.K.
http://www.thekennelclub.org.uk

Beagle Health
http://www.beaglehealth.info/

American Beagle Relief Network
http://www.ambrn.org/

Beagle Welfare
http://www.beaglewelfare.org.uk/

The Scottish Beagle Club
http://www.scottishbeagleclub.org.uk

The Welsh Beagle Club
http://thewelshbeagleclub.co.uk

National Beagle Council (Australia)
http://www.ozbeagles.org/

Beagle Club of Canada
http://www.beagleclubofcanada.com/

Glossary

Abdomen – The surface area of a dog's body lying between the chest and the hindquarters also referred to as the belly.

Allergy – An abnormally sensitive reaction to substances including pollens, foods, or microorganisms. May be present in humans or animals with similar symptoms including, but not limited to, sneezing, itching, and skin rashes.

Anal glands – Glands located on either side of a dog's anus used to mark territory. May become blocked and require treatment by a veterinarian.

Arm – On a dog, the region between the shoulder and the elbow is referred to as the arm or the upper arm.

Back – That portion of a dog's body that extends from the withers (or shoulder) to the croup (approximately the area where the back flows into the tail.)

Bitch – The appropriate term for a female dog.

Blooded – An accepted reference to a pedigreed dog.

Breed – A line or race of dogs selected and cultivated by man from a common gene pool to achieve and maintain a characteristic appearance and function.

Breed standard – A written "picture" of a perfect specimen of a given breed in terms of appearance, movement, and behavior as formulated by a parent organization, for example, the American Kennel Club or in Great Britain, The Kennel Club.

Brows – The contours of the frontal bone that form ridges above a dog's eyes.

Buttocks – The hips or rump of a dog.

Castrate – The process of removing a male dog's testicles.

Chest – That portion of a dog's trunk or body encased by the ribs.

Coat – The hair covering a dog. Most breeds have both an outer coat and an undercoat.

Come into Season – The point at which a female dog becomes fertile for purposes of mating.

Congenital – Any quality, particularly an abnormality, present at birth.

Crate – Any portable container used to house a dog for transport or provided to a dog in the home as a "den."

Crossbred – Dogs are said to be crossbred when each of their parents is of a different breed.

Dam – A term for the female parent.

Dew Claw – The dew claw is an extra claw on the inside of the leg. It is a rudimentary fifth toe.

Euthanize – The act of relieving the suffering of a terminally ill animal by inducing a humane death, typically with an overdose of anesthesia.

Fancier – Any person with an exceptional interest in purebred dogs and the shows where they are exhibited.

Groom – To make a dog's coat neat by brushing, combing, or trimming.

Harness - A cloth or leather strap shaped to fit the shoulders and chest of a dog with a ring at the top for attaching a lead. An alternative to using a collar.

Haunch Bones – Terminology for the hip bones of a dog.

Haw – The membrane inside the corner of a dog's eye known as the third eyelid.

Head – The cranium and muzzle of a dog.

Hip Dysplasia – A condition in dogs due to a malformation of the hip resulting in painful and limited movement of varying degrees.

Hindquarters – The back portion of a dog's body including the pelvis, thighs, hocks, and paws.

Hock – Bones on the hind leg of a dog that form the joint between the second thigh and the metatarsus. Known as the dog's true heel.

Lead – Any strap, cord, or chain used to restrain or lead a dog. Typically attached to a collar or harness. Also called a leash.

Litter – The puppy or puppies from a single birth or "whelping."

Muzzle – That portion of a dog's head lying in front of the eyes and consisting of the nasal bone, nostrils, and jaws.

Neuter – To castrate or spay a dog thus rendering them incapable of reproducing.

Pedigree – The written record of a pedigreed dog's genealogy. Should extend to three or more generations.

Puppy – Any dog of less than 12 months of age.

Separation Anxiety – The anxiety and stress suffered by a dog left alone for any period of time.

Sire – The accepted term for the male parent.

Spay – The surgery to remove a female dog's ovaries to prevent conception.

Whelping – Term for the act of giving birth to puppies.

Withers – The highest point of a dog's shoulders.

Lightning Source UK Ltd.
Milton Keynes UK
UKHW031335190619
344611UK00020B/301/P